CONS
OF SI CE

CONSPIRACY OF SILENCE

HOW SCOT YOUNG'S FATAL FALL IN LONDON EXPOSED AN INTERNATIONAL WEB OF UNEXPLAINED DEATHS

GORDON BOWERS

JOHN BLAKE

Published by
John Blake Publishing Limited
3 Bramber Court, 2 Bramber Road
London W14 9PB

www.johnblakepublishing.co.uk

www.facebook.com/johnblakebooks **f**
twitter.com/jblakebooks **t**

First published in paperback in 2015

ISBN: 978-1-78418-602-9

British Library Cataloguing-in-Publication Data:

A catalogue record for this book is available from the British Library.

Design by www.envydesign.co.uk

Printed in Great Britain by CPI Group (UK) Ltd

1 3 5 7 9 10 8 6 4 2

Papers used by John Blake Publishing are natural, recyclable products made
from wood grown in sustainable forests. The manufacturing processes conform
to the environmental regulations of the country of origin.

CONTENTS

INTRODUCTION

THE MYSTERIOUS DEATH OF SCOT YOUNG

'The rich are different,' novelist F. Scott Fitzgerald is supposed to have said. To which his friend Ernest Hemingway was said to have replied: 'Yes, they have more money.'

This never happened, apparently. Those who know about these things say the exchange was entirely apocryphal. It was made up from two real quotes. In Fitzgerald's 1926 short story 'The Rich Boy', he wrote:

> Let me tell you about the very rich. They are different from you and me. They possess and enjoy early, and it does something to them, makes them soft where we are hard, and cynical where we are trustful, in a way that, unless you were born rich, it is very difficult to understand. They think, deep in their hearts, that they are better than we are because we had to discover the compensations and refuges of life for ourselves. Even when they enter deep

into our world or sink below us, they still think that they are better than we are. They are different.

Then, when the original version of Hemingway's short story 'The Snows of Kilimanjaro' was published in *Esquire* magazine in 1936, one passage read:

The rich were dull and they drank too much, or they played too much backgammon. They were dull and they were repetitious. He remembered poor Scott Fitzgerald and his romantic awe of them and how he had started a story once that began, 'The very rich are different from you and me.' And how someone had said to Scott, Yes, they have more money. But that was not humorous to Scott. He thought they were a special glamorous race and when he found they weren't it wrecked him as much as any other thing that wrecked him.

Apparently, Fitzgerald was offended by this and when 'The Snows of Kilimanjaro' was republished in volume form the name 'Julian' was substituted for his.

I mention this not to give this book a literary kick-off and not because Fitzgerald was another Scott, albeit with two ts; but because the book will give you the chance to make up your mind who is right – Fitzgerald or Hemingway. Are the rich really different? Or do they just have more money?

The life and untimely death of Scot Young tell us bucketloads about what it is to be rich. Although he started out poor in the backstreets of Dundee, little is known of that part of his life. His grieving parents have not spoken to the press and few who knew him then have come forward. The mystery that surrounds him now was a mantle even then.

INTRODUCTION

Indeed, little was known of him even when he soared like a shooting star into the firmament of the super-rich, before coming crashing to earth again – both metaphorically and, tragically, physically.

He only became known to the public when the reporting restrictions at the Family Law Court were dropped some way into what turned out to be one of the longest divorce proceedings in the history of the British legal system. In the courtroom, the figures that were bandied about were staggering. There were millions, sometimes billions, along with all the trappings of seemingly limitless wealth – the diamonds, yachts, private jets, mansions, Porsches, Ferraris, haute cuisine, exotic holidays and, of course, supermodels. Not only that, he was surrounded by others of similar – if not greater – wealth.

Then, suddenly, it was all gone. Nobody knows where. Nobody is saying. But still Scot and his buddies seemed to continue to live the high life. They still lived in mansions or million-pound apartments, living and dying with pockets stuffed full of cash.

Scot Young's tragically short life gives us a glimpse into another world where, perhaps, the people are different. They certainly do not have the concerns of us ordinary mortals – paying our taxes and putting food on the table. They pay more for a meal that we earn in a month and can raise a mortgage that is more than you or I could earn in several lifetimes.

But are they happy? That does not seem to be a consideration. Some of them seem to be very damaged. In fact, a circle of people around Scot Young died in mysterious circumstances. As did Young himself. They were, it seems, members of a Ring of Death.

Now that Young is dead, the chink through which we observed this secret world has closed. The gilded portals of this Gatsbyesque universe are slammed shut and the survivors have closed ranks. Even during the divorce case and the various inquests, they fought tooth and nail against appearing in court. When they did, their answers were less than illuminating. Scot's entire set, it seems, is infected with collective amnesia.

Nevertheless, we are in familiar territory. Young and his circle inhabited Mayfair, Knightsbridge and country houses – just the places Agatha Christie and others of her ilk have led us to expect a murder, or other nefarious goings-on. Who we need on the case is Hercule Poirot. Who we have is Inspector Japp.

The plodding policemen from Scotland Yard came to the conclusion that there was 'nothing suspicious' about the death of Scot Young, when any armchair detective knows that there is suspicion written all over it. Not only that, there are all the other elements of a crime drama. There are mysterious murders, unconvincing suicides, spies, gangsters, drug smugglers, money launderers, con-men, battling blondes, celebrities, famous chefs, glitzy restaurants and night clubs, conniving tycoons, foreign magnates, private eyes, political intrigue, jealousy and greed. Only this isn't a murder mystery; it's real life.

It seems to me that enough has come out about the glittering world that Young inhabited to develop a number of plausible theories about how he met his end. The clues must all be there. It is only a question of figuring it out.

The problem is, of course, that Young himself went to a great deal of trouble to cover his tracks as he went. He hid everything he was doing in off-shore tax havens, sham companies and shell banks. Everyone he dealt with was as secretive as he was. The police, private detectives, forensic accounts, Her Majesty's Revenue & Customs, bankruptcy courts, legal trustees and High Court judges have not been able to untangle the web he spun. Neither have I. But I have done all I can to lay out the evidence as straightforwardly as possible. Attempting to wrestle too much with the detail may result in not seeing the wood for the trees.

While you are trying to solve this 'murder' mystery, don't forget to spend a moment or two to luxuriate in the lifestyles presented here that otherwise you can only dream of. Are the rich really different? You are about to find out.

GORDON BOWERS, LONDON

CHAPTER 1

THE FALL

On the evening of 8 December 2014 the shattered body of bankrupt property tycoon Scot Young was found impaled on the railings sixty feet below his £3 million luxury penthouse apartment in Montagu Square, Marylebone, in central London. He had suffered horrendous injuries after falling four storeys. His mutilated corpse was discovered by fellow residents at 5 pm that Monday afternoon. The police quickly screened the gruesome scene from onlookers. Firefighters had to cut through the railings with an angle grinder before the body could be removed.

'It was a horrific scene,' said fifty-seven-year-old Gary Sutton who was working nearby. 'The police were visibly shocked – one said it was the worst thing he had seen on the job. It was all very distressing.'

It was just as horrifying for passers-by.

'I had to divert my eyes,' another witness said. 'The police had covered the body but I could see from behind that he was on the spike because I could see his feet dangling towards the basement floor. It was horrible.'

Young's horrific death plunge seemed to have come direct from a gangster movie, where mobsters are apt to fling their hapless victims from high buildings. Even good guys such as James Bond or Sherlock Holmes at the Reichenbach Falls had been known to despatch their foes into vertiginous oblivion. But, strangely, Scotland Yard said they were not treating it as suspicious. Soon they were under pressure to change their minds.

Young was already a figure – albeit enigmatic – in the press. He was one of the principal players in what the media was calling the 'biggest divorce case of the century'. If that was not enough to pique the interest of the Metropolitan Police, Young also had connections with the Russian mafia and the most notorious London crime syndicate since the Kray twins were banged up in 1968. The press coverage of Young's fatal dive was intense. His fiancée, American model and reality-TV star Noelle Reno, was said to be heartbroken.

Curiously, the death plunge narrowly avoided being filmed. Scot Young had featured on the Bravo Channel's *Ladies of London*, which had wrapped up just weeks before he died. Noelle Reno was one of the stars of the show. The American-born blonde featured alongside former supermodel Caprice, celebrity shopper and Prince Andrew's ex Caroline Stanbury, the late Alexander McQueen's muse Annabelle Neilson, Lady Julie Montagu and other US socialites who had crossed the pond. Young had even proposed to her during the making of the American TV show. The final episode had just aired and was repeated on ITV hours after he was found dead. This was the stuff Jackie Collins's novels are made of.

THE FALL

Though there were rumours that the couple had split, Ms Reno remained suitably abject over her lover's death.

'I am distraught by the sudden loss of my best friend and ask that you give me the respect and privacy I need to grieve in peace,' she told the press.

However, just the night before Young had met his untimely end, she had tweeted: 'No matter what the day throws, I know I can handle it if my day starts with meditation (even if it's day #4 of insane xmas parties!!).'

The words could hardly have been more ill chosen.

Fifty-two-year-old Scot Young was once one of Britain's wealthiest men and had made a reported £2 billion as what his ex-wife had described as a 'fixer for the super-rich'. A poor boy from a working-class background, he once boasted a 118-foot yacht berthed in Monaco. He globetrotted in a private jet and owned a fleet of luxury cars, along with at least six palatial homes in key locations. One was in Eaton Square, Belgravia, one of London's most exclusive postcodes, though when he was in town he would often stay in the five-star Lanesborough Hotel in Knightsbridge, just around the corner.

His £21-million mansion in Oxfordshire, Woodperry House, was described as 'Buckingham Palace in miniature'. There he was waited on by teams of servants like a Bond villain. With associates, he owned a complete terrace of six stucco-fronted townhouses in Regent's Park and an investment portfolio of stocks and shares in gas and oil companies that netted him around £2 million a year. He also had businesses that paid him a similar amount in commission. Poor he was not. His total fortune was estimated at a conservative £400 million – though his ex-wife believed that it was much, much more. And he liked to spend it.

His clique of wealthy friend included millionaire retailer Sir

Philip Green, *X Factor* entrepreneur Simon Cowell and Richard Caring, owner of the up-market restaurant The Ivy, the Soho House and Annabel's nightclub. Exiled Russian oligarch Boris Berezovsky was also part of the glittering inner circle.

However, while at first supportive, Young's super-rich friends began to give him a wide berth when their own finances came under scrutiny during his acrimonious six-year High Court divorce battle.

While his ex-wife Michelle was eventually awarded over £20 million – none of which he paid – she claimed he had millions more stashed off-shore. During their last months together, they had lived in a £3.5-million beach house in Miami, dined in the finest restaurants and employed a small army of servants and housekeepers. They had driven fabulous cars, the sort that even Jeremy Clarkson only dreams of. Michelle dripped with the most expensive jewellery, while Young wore a £70,000 watch – one of hundreds in his personal collection.

But the dead man was now, apparently, skint. Not only was he poverty-stricken, but he maintained he was over £27 million in debt. The story was that he had invested his huge fortune in a disastrous property deal in Moscow. Every penny, he said, had disappeared down this financial black hole. He was boracic. However, his supermodel girlfriend was not even slightly fazed by his impecunity. Indeed, she was sympathetic to his plight. In an interview, Ms Reno had said, unfortunately in retrospect, that his sudden loss of his wealth 'kills him'.

Having flown so high, his financial melt-down had been a blow he had had trouble coming to terms with.

'He still can't deal with it,' she said. 'It has been so traumatic for him.'

Nevertheless, Ms Reno had stood by him.

The news of Young's death, also left aggrieved ex-wife

Michelle Young, mother of their two children, twenty-one-year-old Scarlet and Sasha, nineteen, distraught. For six long years she had pursued him through the courts and his unexpected death presented yet another, perhaps insurmountable, obstacle to her claiming what she believed was her due. Her dead husband had never revealed where the millions had gone. Now he was silenced forever. And there were the children to consider.

When the divorce case had hit the headlines, she had been voluble. Long interviews had been granted to the newspapers, who had run supportive profiles. Now, understandably, she could only be contacted through the intercom of her model apartment block in her home in Victoria, SW1.

'I am devastated,' she told an inquisitive journalist. 'I just have to look after my children and make sure they are OK. It is a very difficult time for us all. I am with my daughters and we have been to hell and back. We are just in shock, we don't know what to say... I just want to be left alone.'

Young's death, perhaps, was not a complete surprise for her. She had previously claimed her ex-husband had attempted suicide during their bitter divorce court battle. He had been checked into the Priory clinic, the celebrity rehab retreat, for treatment and, on his own admission. he had twice been sectioned under the Mental Health Act.

However, there was no mention of a suicide note and Young had not deliberately sought out a high building to jump off. He and Ms Reno had moved into the Marylebone duplex outside which he died a few months earlier. It was in an area they liked and was an agreeable location to set up home together.

For people of their standing, the place was suitably swish. Next door to the former home of Ringo Starr, it attracted a rent of around £8,000 a month, but a rich pal had agreed to pick up the tab. Otherwise, it was secure. Opposite the Swedish embassy and next door to the Swiss embassy, there would be armed police in the street day and night. And it was cosy. Noelle said it would be a 'happy little home for our happy little life'.

The couple had been together for five years before they got engaged, though throughout that time their relationship was constantly overshadowed by his high-profile divorce case. When her reality-TV show started in June 2014 she said that she would not be getting married any time soon, but had planned the event down to the last detail.

'I would not be capable of organising a wedding at this moment,' she told *OK!* magazine. Originally from Seattle, the thirty-year-old blonde worked as a designer and entrepreneuse, after a career in acting and modelling.

'I'm used to running production and doing events for my businesses,' she said, 'so I don't think that I will freak out. Also my wedding doesn't need to be my most beautiful day. I'm kind of used to having my picture out there, I'm now on a freaking reality-TV show, I don't need all of the attention.'

She also said that the wedding was going to be 'one big festival party' with great DJs. It was not to be.

In an interview with Bravo, Noelle said she had fallen in love with Scot because he 'has a confidence and protective nature that seduced me'.

'Remember, I'm living alone in a foreign country,' she said. 'Over the period I've known him his confidence has dwindled as he's been stripped of his dignity and privacy by all the divorce has brought. Nonetheless, he continues to be massively supportive of me in everything I do and in every aspect of my life. The fact that he is loyal, respectful, and empowering of women is paramount with me.'

Clearly, Scot Young was well liked. After he died, a number

of mourners turned up to lay flowers outside his flat, against the board where the fatal railings had been. A friend named Sam Cash left a note with his floral tribute that read: 'Sorry it had to end this way. You will be forever remembered and live long in the hearts of those who knew you.'

A young woman also left a tribute that read: 'My Darling Scottie, no words. I have loved you since we met eleven years ago. You have broken my heart. XXX LP. Rest in Peace.'

On another bunch, there was a note that said: 'For Scot. Today I didn't only lose my best friend's dad, I really did lose one of my idols. Will miss you Scot & no matter what was mentioned, I could always tell you were a good guy...'

Some came from as far away as Florida.

A friend who came to pay his respects said that Scot Young was a great man and a great father who had been let down by the British legal system. And a family friend said: 'Scot Young was an idol and an inspiration for people who came from underprivileged backgrounds.'

The man, smartly dressed in a blue suit, said he had known Young's daughter for four years: 'He was a good guy at heart. He was definitely someone to look up to. He was an inspiration to anyone who wasn't from a privileged background. He was a self-made man. He's a good idol. He taught me to work hard and never give up; that's why it came to me as a shock.'

When asked if Young's death was a result of his court battle, the man said: 'There were other issues.'

A local man, who paid his respects by laying a white lily at the boarded-up railings, said: 'I live round the corner and saw the aftermath of what happened. It was a pretty grisly scene, so brutal. I saw it was Scot Young in the news and decided to bring a flower out of respect. It's such a human tragedy.'

Others were not so sympathetic. A well-dressed woman,

who said she was a friend of Scot Young's ex-wife Michelle, called his death 'divine justice', saying: 'Now his wife will get the money he owed her.'

Refusing to give her name, the middle-aged woman told the *Daily Mail*: 'It's both good and bad news. Now she can finally go after his hidden assets. His money must be somewhere. It will finally all come out now and the courts will be able to pursue them now and she will be able to cash in on it. She knew he had money somewhere yet he refused to give her what she was rightfully owed. Perhaps this is divine justice. I've known Michelle for years and I knew he was hiding money from her, that's why she battled him in court for six years. Divorces are hard and she has suffered a lot. Now the government will be able to pursue his assets and she'll get the £25 million he owed her.'

Then, smiling, she took photographs of the place where Scot had died, remarking, callously, that she had seen Young smoking several times.

'Maybe Scot fell out of the window while having a cigarette,' she said.

Neighbours said he was alone in the flat at the time, but Ms Reno said she had been in the property earlier in the day. One mourner laying flowers cast doubt on what had happened there.

'We don't know if it is suicide yet,' he said.

There was also a dispute over the money. One associate of Mr Young's said: 'I hope this makes people realise now that there was no money, he didn't have any money. It is very unpleasant.'

Another friend hinted that the opposite was true, saying that Scot was depressed because he had millions stashed abroad but had no way to get his hands on them.

The police, naturally, avoided all speculation. A spokesman

for Scotland Yard said simply that the Metropolitan Police had been called to Montagu Square at 17.18 hrs on Monday, 8 December, due to reports of a man having 'fallen from a fourth-floor window'. The spokesman added: 'A man, believed aged in his early fifties, was pronounced dead at the scene. The death is not being treated as suspicious at this time.'

Many had their doubts. In less than a week, *The Sunday Times* was revealing Young's links to the Russian mafia and the notorious Islington-based crime gang, the Adams family. Even Kremlin-backed Russian radio station Vesti FM and official newspaper *Rossiyskaya Gazeta* were asking: 'Did he jump or was he pushed?'

It was soon the question everyone was asking.

CHAPTER 2

THE RISE

The globetrotting billionaire began life in 1962 in a four storey tenement at Number 8, Clepington Street in a rundown part of Dundee. His father, Duncan Young, was a former Dundee United full-back, back in the days when a professional footballer's wages were counted in hundreds rather than millions of pounds. Later, after the end of his soccer career, he found it difficult to find work. With his wife Betsy, he had just one child, Scot, who was brought into the world in the shadow of Tannadice, Dundee United's stadium.

Little is known of Scot's early life. After his death, his parents avoided the press and no childhood friends came forward. Clearly, he did not do well at school. He left at sixteen with few qualifications. After a few years promoting pop bands and local clubs, where he seemed to have made some unsavoury connections, he moved south where got involved in the property boom of the late 1980s. However, his professional

11

life had not really got underway and he was still relatively poor when, in 1987, he met twenty-six-year-old Michelle Orwell, the daughter of a successful Essex businessman.

Michelle was youngest of three children. Her father, Terence, ran a thriving business dealing with high-end electrical goods. Though her parents were not short of money, she had attended the local comprehensive.

'Even though my father did well,' she said, 'he said he wanted us to live in the real world, which I would say is a good thing.'

Although not academic, Michelle was creative and entre-preneurial. At the age of eighteen, with her father's help, she set up a company sourcing fashion collections in Italy and Paris, which she then sold to a private client base in the UK. She gained a reputation for being 'tenacious, ambitious and hard-working, but also happy-go-lucky'. The business flourished and she was already well established when she met Scot.

'He was originally from Dundee and when we met he said he was in the property business,' said Michelle. 'But he didn't explain too much about it. He was always very secretive, even then.'

Nevertheless, she found his personality magnetic. He was also 'assertive'; his poor background, she thought, gave him the drive to do well.

'He was young, charismatic and ambitious, but I fell in love with Scot's sense of humour,' she said. 'He had an ego but, over the years, as he became more successful, money and power inflated it.'

He was also romantic.

'He told me within two days of meeting me that he wanted us to marry and have children,' she said.

Although they did not rush into marriage, she was not against the idea and thought they were well suited as they were both 'fiery and stubborn'. Clearly, they both had an entrepreneurial streak. The problem was, when they first met, he had no money.

'He was just breaking into the property business and it was me who gave him some start-up cash,' she said.

Her father also gave him financial help as well as important introductions. Even so, they could not afford to set up home on their own. Within a few months, he moved in with her at her parents' home in Brentwood – a ten-acre farm where Michelle also bred miniature horses. This was not a problem. Her parents also warmed to Scot and treated him as a son.

'My family are warm and embracing,' Michelle said. 'They knew I was in love and they liked Scot, so we all got on well.'

For Scot, life with the Orwells could hardly had been more different from his own upbringing. Young was the only child of parents who were both only children.

'Being surrounded by a big family was something that he had never had,' Michelle said, 'and it was a new experience for him.'

The family was on hand to help.

'My father helped him in business, introducing him to contacts,' said Michelle, who was still working as a fashion buyer. 'It was through a contact of my father that Scot first met Philip Green.'

Born in 1952 in South London, Green was the son of a property developer. He took over the family company in 1973, before going into the retail trade. He bought a number of clothing firms, which he ran and sold on. He rose to own a number of High Street chains, including JJB Sports, Olympus Sports, Miss Selfridge, Wallis, Warehouse and Freeman. In 2002, with his wife Tina, he took Arcadia, the parent company of Topshop, Dorothy Perkins, Evans and Burton, among others. Along the way, he made a great deal of money. He has a £32-million yacht and a £20-million private jet. At his birthday parties he has been entertained by the likes of Rod Stewart, Tom Jones and Rihanna. His wife bought him a solid gold monopoly set and for his fifty-fifth he flew a hundred guests to the Maldives.

While Green was known for his inventive tax avoidance schemes, he was a government adviser and was knighted in 2006 for his charity work.

Michelle's father also gave Scot money to invest in his business. Michelle invested too. They worked side-by-side in the early days, she insisted.

'Scot controlled the money side of things, which is why there was nothing in my name alone. But we were most definitely a partnership,' she said later.

The property market was booming at the time and they bought houses to renovate and sell on with considerable success. After three years, they moved out of her parents' farm into a home of their own – a Tudor-style house in nearby Theydon Bois that had a swimming pool and tennis court set in a few acres of Essex countryside.

Michelle gave up her career in fashion when she became pregnant with Scarlet in 1992. Around then, Young was arrested for drug trafficking, but he was not convicted. Michelle claimed that he was involved with the Patrick Adams, enforcer of the Adams Family, also known as the Clerkenwell crime syndicate. Patrick, aka 'Patsy', was sentenced to seven years in jail for armed robbery in the 1970s. He was suspected in at least twenty-five gangland murders over a three-year period.

Said to be 'ten times more scary than the Krays', the Adams crime family were thought to be worth between anywhere £80 and £200 million. They called themselves the 'A-Team', after a cheesy American TV crime show of the 1980s. But it was also the name used by the Green Berets for their crack squads who work behind enemy lines.

The family was run by three brothers – Terry, the eldest, Patsy and Sean, aka Tommy – who were brought up on the Barnsbury Council Estate, just a few minutes walk from Tony Blair's home before he moved into Number Ten Downing Street. At school they lent on other kids for their pocket money. Then they went into petty thieving before moving into protection, putting the strong arm on local market traders. Next came armed robbery. The proceeds were invested in local businesses, including mini-cab firms, car washes, and legal and illegal drinking clubs. One – the Ra-RAs in Upper Street – became a favourite haunt of players from the local football team, Arsenal. Soon the Adamses extended their operations south into London's jewellery district, Hatton Garden.

The Adams family, it was said, arranged for the gold from the 1983 Brink's Mat heist, a £26-million bullion robbery at Heathrow Airport, to be melted down and took a cut of the proceeds. What better place to do this than Hatton Garden? This confirmed the Adams as the pre-eminent firm north of the river. Tommy Adams was later prosecuted for his involvement, but walked free with co-defendant Kenneth Noye who was later jailed for murder after a road-rage incident. The police believe that the jury in the Brink's Mat trial had been 'nobbled'.

The money was used to fund a drug-smuggling operation. In 1984, Patsy Adams was arrested for importing 3.5 tons of cannabis, worth an estimated £25 million. This time he was acquitted even though his partner in the venture ended up with an eleven-year sentence when the case finally came to trial in 1993. When Patsy was nicked on fresh drugs charges, the police found a shooter and a complete set of bullet-proof body armour, which Patsy claimed belonged to his wife. Once again, a jury miraculously believed his story.

They used to the money from drugs to bribe policemen and other officials. They also took over clubs in the West End until their empire extended as far as Fulham. Their business methods were simplicity itself. One club owner in West London told Wensley Clarkson, author of *Gang Wars of London*: 'The Adamses sent a couple of their chaps down to see me because they knew I was up to my eyes in debt and they wanted to buy the club for a knockdown price. I didn't argue with them. They chucked me a few grand and I was out the door in minutes. I didn't want any aggro.'

They also moved into the expensive clubs and pubs where free-spending young professionals had developed a nose for cocaine. Even the most respectable club owners found it difficult to get them out. Favoured associates were plied with free drinks and sex, then pressured into co-operation. The alternative was having a gun waved in your face. Mickey, the youngest of the brothers, was convicted of the possession of a firearm in the mid-1980s.

However, back in Islington, they still had deadly rivals – a gang known as the Reillys. There was a flare-up on New Year's Day 1990, when one of the A-Team's lieutenant 'dissed' George Reilly in front of his wife on Islington High Street. Reilly rushed home and grabbed a gun. Returning, he took pot-shots at a carpet shop where the A-Team lieutenant had sought refuge. Luckily, no one was injured. Nevertheless, this was not a matter to be taken lightly.

Two days later, Scot Young's alleged associate Patsy Adams strode into the Prince Alfred in Huntingdon Street, Islington, North London. The boozer was known to locals as 'the quiet house' and was the home turf of their bitter North London enemies, the Reillys. This was a deliberate wind-up.

Patsy Adams knew exactly what the reaction would be. Word quickly got back to the Reillys. They sent four armed men in a red BMW to sort him out. But it was a trap. Two cars full of Adams's soldiers were waiting at the end of the road. As the Beemer turning into Huntingdon Street, it was peppered with shots from pistols and shotguns.

Residents of the surrounding Victorian terraced houses dived for cover as the red limo slammed into reverse. In a wild-west style shoot out bullets chipped off chunks of brickwork and scarred the pavements. Again, it was only a matter of luck that no one was hurt.

The owner of the BMW was John Reilly. A club-owner, he was jailed for thirty months after pleading guilty to violent behaviour at the Old Bailey. As a result, neither he, nor any of the other suspected participants, had to reveal what really happened in Huntingdon Street that night. Nevertheless, the judge at Reilly's trial was convinced he knew who else was involved and described the Adams family in court as 'a group of first-division criminals'.

Patsy was fearless. In 1991, he was suspected of a murder attempt on 'Mad' Frankie Fraser who had been an enforcer for both the Richardsons and the Krays. When Fraser got involved in Turnmills Nite Club that the Adamses were running in Clerkenwell, he was shot on the pavement. Patsy cut off part of Fraser's son David's ear during a fall-out over drugs. And he developed the 'two on a bike' hit, with the man on the pillion wielding the gun. With business being taken care of by trusted lieutenants, Patsy began to spend more time at his holiday home in Marbella, on the Costa del Crime.

Discretion was the better part of valour. They avoided

publicity at all costs. When armed robber turned journalist John McVicar first mentioned them in an article in 1987 he received a visit from a family associate, who politely and firmly extracted a promise not to write about the family in the future. However, when McVicar contravened this agreement and mentioned that one of the gang shot Mad Frankie Fraser the previous August, he received another visit.

'Although I apologised for the breach, the emissary shrugged his shoulders and grimaced mournfully,' said McVicar. '"John," he said, "it saddens me to have to say it, and I hope it won't go any further, but if I were you I'd purchase some portable insurance, get in some target practice and be very careful of big trail bikes in your immediate vicinity."'

McVicar said he explained it was not appropriate for a journalist to carry a gun.

Terry Adams and West Indian enforcer Gilbert Wynter were armed when they were arrested on the way to sort out a dodgy drugs deal in 1992. For years, Wynter was a useful conduit to the Yardie drug gangs of North London. In 1994, he was charged with murdering former British high-jump champion Claude Moseley. Mosley had been called to a house in Stoke Newington to discuss rumours he was short-changing his suppliers, the A-Team. After Mosley produced a gun, Wynter virtually sliced him in half with a Samurai sword.

Though Wynter was charge with the murder, he walked at the Old Bailey when a key witness refused to give testimony and was jailed for contempt of court. Although the judge was forced to acquit Wynter, he was convinced that he had done it, condemning the fact that 'a man who can commit this kind of crime can get away with it'.

Wynter later disappeared amid rumours that he had double-crossed the A-Team. The story was that he was summoned to

Islington where a van was waiting. It was raining heavily and he was wearing an expensive suit. He climbed into the van backwards to keep the rain off it with an umbrella, so he did not see the men who were waiting to kill him.

'If he hadn't been worried about his suit he would have seen who was inside and realised what was up,' said a source. 'He won't be seen again.'

It is thought that he is part of the foundations of the Millennium Dome.

In the early 1990s the Adamses decided to hide their vast profits from criminal activities. They were seen in the plush offices of a top corporate lawyer, discussing deals such as financing the £10 million takeover of Tottenham Hotspur by then manager Terry Venables, plus the £30 million refinancing of the failing London Arena in Docklands, then owned by boxing promoter Frank Warren. None of these deals ever materialised, but the corporate lawyer was kidnapped and held in a Glasgow hotel by some associates of the Adamses. He was returned to London where he was severely beaten. Soon after, he flew to Spain and did not return to the UK for five years.

Another businessman who found himself in debt to the Adams gang hired a former associate of the Krays to sort things out. When he returned, he told the businessman: 'You'd better pay up or they'll 'ave you.'

Property dealer Michael Olymbious was not so lucky. When he went bust owing money to the Adamses, he fled to Cyprus. A few years later, he made a flying visit to London to see his family. The night before he was to return to Cypus, he was getting out of his car when a bullet passed clean through his head.

The Adamses took over Olymbious's Beluga Club in Finchley Road. In 1994, the club was sponsoring a world title fight by

Chris Eubank, but when a tabloid exposed the Adams link, top boxing promoter Barry Hearn pulled out.

According to the Metropolitan Police, two of Scot Young's associates laundered money for the Adamses. It was thought that Young may have done that too. They were not good people to do business with. If anything went wrong, things could get very unhealthy indeed. Certainly they were not above killing those who appeared to cross them. Nevertheless, money was rolling in and no one asked where it was coming from.

Michelle gave birth to Sasha two years later and the couple married in March 1995 at Chelsea Register Office. They were deeply in love.

'We were happy then', she said. 'And when it was good, it was great.'

A wedding photograph shows Michelle, a slim, blonde Jean Shrimpton lookalike signing the register as her curly-haired new husband beams at the camera. The ring, she said, was worth £1 million. The diamond set turned out to be worth £150,000. He said he had bought it from Giraffe.

But there were problems.

'He was very volatile,' said Michelle. But the fault was not on one side only.

'We are both quite fiery and stubborn,' she admitted, 'and I like to defend myself. So sometimes, for the girls' sake, I would try to keep calm, but sometimes we clashed.'

By this time, the property business was expanding rapidly. Michelle used her design skills when they bought houses to renovate. She also had an eye for a bargain and would often find the properties herself.

'We started off together and we made it together,' she said. 'I was a mother and a loyal wife. I also handled the interiors side of the business. I found the properties we bought, I renovated them, I sold them on – on one occasion at a £10 million profit.'

The slim blonde was certainly more than just as a trophy wife.

'I wasn't just a housewife,' she said. 'It is fair to say that I was key to his early success.'

Others confirmed this.

'Although the business was always Scot's, Michelle was heavily involved in its success,' said a friend. 'It was a partnership in every sense. She helped him build the business and his contacts, and put her design skills to use on the renovation side.'

To the outside observer, they were the perfect couple. They were good-looking with a young family, upwardly mobile and clearly destined for great things. But though Michelle had known her husband for six years, she only gradually became aware of a 'darker side' that he had kept hidden away. Soon after they were married, it began to emerge. Though they seemed to be on a golden path to untold riches, he was volatile and prone to bouts of aggression that seemed to come from nowhere.

'He could get very angry for no reason and start throwing things about,' Michelle said. 'But whenever we fought he would apologise afterwards and, like so many women do, I believed that if I loved him enough, he would change. I thought fatherhood would mellow him, but as the stakes in his business got higher, and he started to mix in different circles, the man I fell in love with disappeared completely. I believe you should stick at a marriage, so I tried to make our home a happy place.'

By the mid-nineties, Young's circle of wealthy friend included Sir Tom Hunter, the property and sports goods tycoon who appeared on *The Sunday Times* Rich List as Scotland's first home-grown billionaire. They would holiday on board Hunter's yacht in the Mediterranean. With Tom Hunter and Philip Green, Young moved into business ventures outside property. But Scot was still very secretive and Michelle had little idea of what he was up to

'They made hundreds of millions from a telecoms venture,' she said. 'But I didn't have much of an idea about what exactly they were doing.'

Young's first really big break came in 1997, when he purchased a half share in Dione, a company involved in chip and pin machines. The other half was purchased by a Finnish-born, London-based billionaire property developer and art collector named Chaim 'Poju' Zabludowicz. Owner of the Liechtenstein-registered Tamares investment group, he was on *The Sunday Times* Rich List 2009 as the eighteenth wealthiest person in the UK, with an estimated fortune of £1.5 billion. He was thought to own 40 per cent of the real estate in downtown Las Vegas. His Israeli-based father built a fortune from the defence industry and entertained lavishly on his 120-foot yacht. Poju later bankrolled David Cameron's campaign for the leadership of the Conservative Party. He also funded the Tories to the extent of £129,000.

Zabludowicz and his wife Anita own neighbouring 'his' and 'her' mansions on Bishops Avenue in Hampstead, known locally as 'Billionaires' Row'. The properties, which have a swimming pool, a gym, two cinemas, a wine-tasting venue and a wine cellar, were reportedly the venue for secret talks between Israeli President Shimon Peres and Palestinian President Mahmoud Abbas in 2011.

Money was coming in thick and fast, and the family moved into Woodperry House, a nine-bedroom Palladian mansion on a two-hundred-acre estate in Oxfordshire. Though Young seemed to have limitless supplies of money, his dealings were already complex. Woodperry House was bought with the help of a £2.5 million mortgage and a £1.5 million loan. Again, Michelle takes credit for the move, which turned out to be very profitable.

'I found that property and it proved to be a good buy,' she said. As well as making it their home, they used it as collateral to buy further properties. Four years later, they sold it for £13.5 million.

Largely, though, Michelle was now excluded from the business. Although in the house the family were waited on by a bevy of servants, Michelle liked to be the type of stay-at-home mum her own mother had been. Even with staff, there were plenty of household arrangements to be made.

'I was busy running that and looking after the girls,' she said.

And when it came to Scot's business, she found herself even more outside the loop.

'Although Scot saw Philip and Tom all the time, I only met them a few times socially,' she said. 'When I did meet them, it was just chit-chat. People like Tom Hunter, Philip Green and my husband simply don't discuss business with their wives.'

Another influential friend was director-general of the BBC Mark Thompson, with whom the Youngs regularly dined *en famille*.

'We lived out in the countryside and they were in Oxford,' said Michelle. 'But we were in and out of each other's homes and dined together about once a month. Our favourite place was Raymond Blanc's restaurant, Le Manoir aux Quat'Saisons in Oxfordshire. Scot usually picked up the bill, which was invariably well over £2,000. And he bought their children very expensive gifts – he was generous when he thought someone could be useful to him.'

CONSPIRACY OF SILENCE

The two men had met a few years earlier through the exclusive £8,000-a-term Dragon prep school in Oxfordshire, which their children attended. Otherwise Young, the self-made millionaire from the backstreets of Dundee, and Thompson, the alumnus of the elite Jesuit Stonyhurst College in Lancashire with a first in English from Oxford, seemed to have little in common. Thompson was then boss of Channel 4, but the friendship continued after he took over the BBC in 2004.

Despite his other interests, Young continued investing in property. At one point his property portfolio was estimated to have been worth more than £100 million. In 2004 Lord Andrew Hay, of the up-market estate agency Knight Frank, described him as 'the most important single private client within the UK'. Hay said he had done business with Young for ten years on properties ranging from £2 million to £20 million.

'I personally have been involved in over £60 million of transactions with him,' Hay said.

While friends like Philip Green and Tom Hunter relished the limelight, Young preferred to stay out of the glare of the media and operate under the radar. There was little about him in the press during his seemingly effortless ascent.

'He wasn't one for throwing glitzy parties, but he was extravagant and generous,' said Michelle.

He was not one for stinting himself either. A fan of Dolce & Gabbana, every time they brought out a new collection for men, he would buy the entire range. He spent around £1 million a year on clothes for himself.

His other indulgence was fabulously expensive watches. He bought a new one every time he pulled off a big deal. In the end, it is estimated that he had more than two hundred. He also bought luxury cars whenever he felt like it, sometimes buying a new one every six weeks.

'They only ever flew by private jet and at any one time they had £3 million worth of cars parked in the driveway,' said a friend. These included two £700,000 Mercedes Gullwing cars, the pride of his collection.

'The Youngs weren't just rich, they were super-rich,' said an acquaintance. 'It was a dream existence.'

They were also regulars on the A-list party scene, rubbing shoulders with senior statesmen including former US President Bill Clinton. It seems he may have had some business dealings there too. There was no end to his ambition. Michelle said she had once heard that her husband was 'on the verge of a deal involving Bill Clinton that would make him one of the richest men in the world'.

That does not seem to have come off. But still there was more than enough money to cover their everyday needs. The house was filled with antiques worth more than £4 million. They slept on antique beds that cost £10,000 a piece. Scot was also generous with the girls. His daughters were treated to small battery-powered Jeeps to ride round the estate and Arabian horses. They got Cartier watches for their birthdays. There were frequent family holidays in Capri, New York and Barbados. When they did not go by private jet, they often travelled by Concorde. Back in England, the family would sometimes dine at Le Manoir aux Quat' Saisons as often as twice a week.

'It was an amazing life,' said Michelle.

But as they grew richer, Young became more unstable. Things became almost unbearable.

'There were frequent rows and he humiliated me a lot,' she said. 'He would play the macho man and swear at me in front of workmen, for example, ordering me about and telling me to do this and do that.'

In 2001, the family moved out of Woodperry House and into an equally impressive mansion on the Wentworth Park Estate in Egham, Surrey. But after a couple of months, they returned to Oxfordshire because Sasha and Scarlet missed their schools. The Wentworth Estate was sold to Boris Berezovsky, who was preparing to flee Russia, for over £19 million. This was the beginning of Young's association with the billionaire and it was then that he got involved with the Russians, which may very well have led to his death.

'It was through this sale that the two of them became very close,' said Michelle some years later. 'Again, I don't know what business they did together, but one of our mutual friends told me recently that whenever he sees Scot these days he is always with Boris.'

CHAPTER 3

PROJECT MOSCOW

Boris Berezovsky was at the centre of the deal that Scot Young claimed he lost all his money on. If Young had fallen foul of the Russian mafia, this was the cause of it. Berezovsky had some powerful enemies. Many of his acquaintances met untimely ends and he was certainly the centre of the circle of Young's associates who died mysteriously – the so-called Ring of Death.

Berezovsky had an odd background for an oligarch. He was not a government official, a secret policeman or an entrepreneur. He was a mathematician. The son of a civil engineer, he was born to a Jewish family in Moscow in 1946. At first, he studied forestry, then graduated with a PhD in applied mathematics in 1983. Continuing with his academic work, he published sixteen books and articles, and rose to become a professor at the somewhat sinister-sounding Institute of Control Sciences in Moscow. (In fact, it's a centre for research into engineering control systems, eg vehicle navigation.)

CONSPIRACY OF SILENCE

In 1989, as the Soviet Union began to crumble, he went into business selling cars from the state manufacturer Autovaz. After the collapse of the USSR in 1991, he set up his own company Logovaz. Success in Russia, either then or now, was not possible without a *krysha* or roof – protection not just from the political and security authorities, but also organised crime groups. In the 1990s, these mafia gangs dominated several business sectors, including the sale of cars. Berezovsky's *krysha* was the Chechen crime outfit that fought with rival Slav gangs for control of Moscow. A gunfight occurred outside a Logovaz showroom in 1993. The following year, Berezovsky survived a car bomb, which injured him and killed his driver. He was later accused of helping to fund anti-Kremlin Chechen separatists.

Under the presidency of Boris Yeltsin, he lent money to the state in return for valuable stakes in Autovaz, the state airline Aeroflot, and several oil companies, which he organised into the giant Sibneft. Among his partners in these ventures were Roman Abramovich and Georgian businessman Arkady 'Badri' Patarkatsishvili. Arkady died in suspicious circumstances at Downside Manor, his home in Leatherhead, Surrey, in 2008, after reportedly failing to go through with a deal that would have resulted in him investing $2 billion in the Georgian railways. Patarkatsishvili was Berezovsky's connection to the Chechen mafia and after Patarkatsishvili's death Berezovsky launched a £3 billion legal action against his estate.

Next Berezovsky moved into the media, taking over the television channels ORT and TV6, and the newspapers *Nezavisimaya Gazeta*, *Novye Izvestiya* and *Kommersant*, which he used to support Yeltsin's re-election in 1996. Entering the Davos Pact with fellow oligarchs, he helped bankroll Yelstin's campaign and was behind a plot in Club Logovaz that ousted

Kremlin hardliners. The *New York Times* called Berezovsky the 'public spokesman and chief lobbyist for the new elite'. He then became the Deputy Secretary for Chechnya, in charge of lucrative contracts to reconstruct the war-torn, oil-rich state. By 1998, he was the richest man in Russia. *Forbes* magazines estimated his worth at $3 billion. And he was one of a close-knit circle around Yelstin, known as the 'Family'.

That November, in a televised press conference, five officers of the Russian Federal Security Service, the FSB, led by Lieutenant Colonel Alexander Litvinenko, revealed an alleged plot by their superiors to assassinate Berezovsky. This did not endear him to his boss at the FSB, Vladimir Putin. As a result, Litvinenko was dismissed from the FSB. Putin said: 'I fired Litvinenko and disbanded his unit… because FSB officers should not stage press conferences. This is not their job. And they should not make internal scandals public.'

Evading arrest, Litvinenko and his family fled to Turkey where he applied for asylum at the US embassy. When this was denied, he flew to the UK where he was granted asylum in 2001.

Berezovsky and the Family backed Putin to take over from Yeltsin as president. In the early 1990s, as deputy mayor of St Petersburg, Putin had helped Logovaz establish a dealership there. They became close personal friends. They went skiing together in Switzerland. Putin attended Berezosky's wife's birthday party and visited his villa in Spain five times. Berezovsky and Abramovich were seen together at an invitation-only inauguration event for Putin. But soon after they fell out. Within three months, Berezovsky had resigned from the Russian parliament, the Duma, in protest against Putin's moves to re-establish an authoritarian regime. He also attacked Putin's handling of the *Kursk* disaster. When the nuclear submarine sank, Putin refused foreign help and 118 crewmen died.

Putin responded by saying he would not tolerate criticism of his government by media controlled by the oligarchs. He warned Berezovsky: 'The state has a cudgel in its hands that you use to hit just once, but on the head. We haven't used this cudgel yet. We've just brandished it... [But] the day we get really angry, we won't hesitate to use it.'

Russian prosecutors re-opened a fraud investigation involving Aeroflot and Berezovsky was called in for questioning. He was abroad at the time and chose exile in England rather than return. His associate in Moscow, Nikolai Glushkov, was arrested. Berezosky, Patarkatsishvili and Vladimir Gusinsky, another exiled oligarch, lost most of their media holdings. Berezovsky and Patarkatsishvili sold their stake in ORT to Roman Abramovich, who then ceded editorial control to the Kremlin. Berezovsky maintained that part of the deal was to have Glushkov freed, but he was not released.

In Britain, Berezovsky began an active campaign to desta-bilise Putin. He was joined by Litvinenko who, in his book *Blowing Up Russia*, claimed the Russian security services were implicated in a series of apartment block bombings in 1999 that killed more than three hundred people, part of a coup to bring Putin to power. He also claimed that FSB agents trained al-Qaeda leaders in Dagestan and were involved in the 9/11 attacks. In 2002, he was convicted *in absentia* in Russia and sentenced to three and a half years for corruption. Fellow FSB agent Mikhail Trepashkin, then in jail, warned him that an FSB unit had been assigned to assassinate him.

In a series of newspaper articles, Litvinenko claimed that the FSB were complicit in the 2002 Moscow theatre siege, the 2004 Beslan school massacre and numerous other terrorist attacks. According to Litvinenko, former prime minister of Italy and president of the European Commission Romano Prodi had also worked for the KGB. However, perhaps his most damaging allegation was that Vladimir Putin, by then president of the Russian Federation, had ordered the assassination of dissident journalist Anna Politkovskaya. There were wilder accusations – that Putin was involved in drug running, even that he was a paedophile.

On 1 November 2006, Litvinenko met two former KGB officers, Andrei Lugovoy and Dmitry Kovtun, in the Pine Bar of the Millennium Hotel in Mayfair. Then he had lunch with Italian nuclear-waste expert Mario Scaramella at Itsu, a sushi restaurant in Piccadilly. Afterwards he fell ill. Suffering from diarrhoea and vomiting, he found he could not walk and was taken to hospital. It was thought he had been poisoned with thallium. His hair fell out and a picture of him on his deathbed was released. 'I want the world to see what they did to me,' Litvinenko said. In a final statement, he blamed Vladimir Putin for his death.

On 22 November, Alexander Litvinenko died of heart failure. After he was dead, his body was found to contain more than two hundred times the lethal dose of the radioactive element polonium. Detectives from Scotland Yard found they could trace three trails of radioactive polonium – connecting Litvinenko, Lugovoy and Kovtun. Passengers on board the planes Lugovy and Kovtun had flown back to Moscow on were warned to contact the Department of Health. Meanwhile, the UK Atomic Weapons Establishment traced the source of the polonium to the Ozersk nuclear power plant, near the city of Chelyabinsk in Russia.

The British government requested the extradition of Lugovy to face charges relating to Litvinenko's death. The request was denied. Kovtun was under investigation by the German authorities for suspected plutonium smuggling, but Germany dropped the case in 2009.

There can be little doubt why Litvinenkov was killed. Two days after he died, representative Sergei Abeltsev told the Russian Duma: "The deserved punishment reached the traitor. I am confident that this terrible death will be a serious warning to traitors of all colours, wherever they are located. In Russia, they do not pardon treachery. I would recommend citizen Berezovsky to avoid any food at the commemoration for his accomplice Litvinenko."

After US security analyst Paul Joyal alleged that Litvinenko had been killed as a warning to all critics of the Putin government, he was shot outside his home in Maryland. Clearly, Boris Berezovsky moved in dangerous circles.

This did not bother Michelle though. As usual, Scot kept her at arm's length from his business dealings, though she did meet the oligarch socially.

'I met Boris on a few occasions,' she said. 'He took us to Le Manoir to thank us for the house. Over dinner he gave me a Fabergé brooch and Scot Fabergé cufflinks. I also met him at a charity function at Windsor Castle but I never really got to know him. He was like the others in Scot's inner circle.'

Some thought that the dealings between the two men were innocent enough. One millionaire acquaintance said: 'Scot's a fixer. He helps wealthy people. If someone needs a house, he'll get them a house. If they need a nice car, he'll get them a car. His main business was peddling expensive properties. He would live in them and then sell them on.' Berezovsky was a special client of Young's though. 'He sometimes turned up in Boris's office with plans of the latest house he was selling.'

Michelle was convinced that her husband was more deeply involved than that and, while she was never privy to the business deals they cooked up, she was sure that huge sums of money were involved.

'It amuses me when I read how Scot was this fixer who would find cars and houses for oligarchs,' she said. 'If anything, he was Boris's equal. And he was far too grand simply to find cars for his rich friends.'

In fact, he gave them away. As a thank you for a favour, he would buy a pal a Bentley or a Ferrari. He was a regular customer of Jack Barclay, the luxury-car dealership in Berkeley Square, Mayfair. No gift was too large for those Scot Young did business with.

Michelle got her share too. Young once bought her a Range Rover filled with couture dresses by designer Maria Grachvogel worth tens of thousands of pounds and his fortieth birthday present to her was £1 million of Graff diamond jewellery. She lived in the lap of luxury.

'We had a small army of housekeepers, cooks and drivers,' said Michelle. 'We had weekly deliveries from the food hall at Harrods. We wanted for nothing,' admits Michelle, who now does her weekly shop at Sainsbury's. 'We're talking the kind of money that makes anything, absolutely anything, possible.'

The marriage was not close and her husband had an eye for other women, but there was no shortage of housekeeping money.

'There was really no limit to what I could spend,' she said. 'I could have anything I wanted. I never had fewer than three luxury cars, including a Hummer just to take my dogs to the vet.'

Later she said that the line about her weekly shop being delivered by Harrods was a myth conjured up by journalists.

'That is really not me,' she explained. 'I like to go and buy my shopping and see what I am getting. I am passionate about food so I would go to the delicatessen or to the market for fresh fruit and vegetables. I still do that – whatever I am doing in life, I am always hands-on.'

Nevertheless, it was clear that no expense was spared.

According to her own account, she continued to play the old-fashioned wife. Despite their wealth, 'I ran his bath and cooked his supper,' she said, 'and I never had nannies, I have my mum to thank for that. She was a fantastic hands-on mother and I wanted to be the same for my girls.'

But disturbing things were going on in the background, and Michelle's growing disquiet brought new strains to the marriage. One episode in 2005 brought it almost to the point of collapse.

Michelle was at home with the girls when three of Scot's cars – a Mercedes, a Porsche Turbo and a Porsche Cayenne – were stolen. She did not see what happened, but when she noticed that the cars were gone, she checked the CCTV and saw that the robbers were wearing balaclavas and they were armed.

Terrified, she called the police. They were there when Young came home. He was very aggressive and started screaming, blaming Michelle for the theft.

'My cars, my cars,' he yelled. 'Why didn't you fucking stop them?'

The policeman tried to calm things down, telling him he should be grateful that none of the family been hurt. The cars seemed to be more important to him than the lives of his family. Michelle found the whole thing very upsetting. She thought about leaving him. But, by then, they had been together for eighteen years and married for over ten. They had two children together and a luxurious lifestyle that was not easy to give up.

Young did not want to lose his wife and children either, so Scot gave Michelle and the girls a choice – move into Easton

Neston, one of Britain's finest country estates, then on the market for £50 million, or to a luxury beach house in Miami.

'We chose the fresh start in Miami,' said Michelle. It was a place they had often visited and they enjoyed the weather there. They bought a $5.5million beachfront home, where they kept three Porsches. But this was only to be 'a base' while they searched for somewhere more substantial.

The move was not going to mend the marriage though. Within weeks of arriving in Florida, Young returned to Britain, telling Michelle he was 'negotiating a very big Russian deal, a £2-billion shopping and office development that he called Project Moscow'.

He was away for three months, though he paid a flying visit to Miami for two days in January 2006 to celebrate his birthday. But it was plain something was wrong.

'What was strange was how moved he was by the fuss we made of him on his birthday,' said Michelle. 'He had to leave the room on one occasion because he was crying.'

She had spotted that something was up a month earlier.

'At Christmas, he made an incredible fuss of us,' she said. 'Even by his standards he was generous. He gave me a Damien Hirst sketch he'd bought at auction – outbidding Hugh Grant – and a diamond necklace. The girls got Cartier watches and Louis Vuitton luggage.'

Three months later, she got a call from a solicitor tell, her that her husband had lost all his money, had attempted suicide and was in the Priory. She was incredulous.

'I couldn't take it in,' she said. 'I couldn't believe it.'

A week later he came back to Miami, saying he had lost everything on Project Moscow.

'From then on things spiralled out of control,' said Michelle. 'I knew things weren't good... That's when the nightmare began.'

Everything, including the £4 million of antiques, was repossessed. The money was drained from all their accounts and she was left with nothing. Young was very agitated and spent much of his time in the garden on his mobile phone, out of earshot.

She later said in an interview: 'Moving money around quietly and undetected is what my husband does. And since working for the Russians, Scot has learned a lot more about how to operate discreetly.'

Michelle was beginning to have her doubts about what he had told her about Project Moscow. She said she then found evidence on his laptop that he was hiding away much of his wealth. For Michelle, this was the final straw and she turned to her daughters for support.

'The girls wanted me to leave him,' she said.

Despite their lavish lifestyle, the marriage had failed emotionally long before it fell apart financially, she conceded.

'He had been having affairs, which I found out about afterwards,' she said. 'I loved him, so I suppose I didn't see through it.'

Even so, it wasn't all bad, though it was clear that the end was nigh.

'Although there were some happy times in our marriage, it wasn't easy most of the time. I became wary of my husband,' she said. 'More than once, I found the phone numbers of other women, and he made the usual excuses, but I sensed that something was very wrong.'

Eventually it proved too much to bear.

'I lost all trust in him and was convinced he had other women in his life,' she said. 'In the end, my girls begged me to leave.'

On 5 November 2006, they back to London with what money

Michelle could scrape together and a suitcase of clothes. They stayed at a hotel for two months, then rented a townhouse by Regent's Park, selling her Graff diamonds to pay the rent.

The following year, she discovered that his infidelity was institutionalised. He was living in one of their homes in Regent's Park with another woman, who later went on to marry one of his friends. In June 2007 she filed for divorce on the grounds of unreasonable behaviour. Then a bitter court battle began – not over the divorce itself, but over money.

'When news of our divorce hit the papers,' Michelle said, 'several people who knew my husband socially have said they saw him with so many other women over the years that they hadn't realised he was married.'

By 2009, when the reporting restrictions on the divorce case were lifted, the *Daily Mail* found Michelle Young searching inside her purse for change while shopping in Morrisons. She was still living in the townhouse near Regent's Park and clad in designer clothes. But she was watching every penny in the struggle to make ends meet.

CHAPTER 4

THE WRONGED WIFE

Proceedings in the family courts are shrouded in secrecy, which would have suited the secretive Scot Young. However, in June 2009, the judge, Mr Justice Charles, made a special order allowing the press to report the hearing. This was because Mr Young was not co-operating with proceedings.

Divorcing couples are required to fill out Form E – a full financial disclosure. But the judge said Young's Form E was 'so uninformative as to be nearly useless'. He also feared that Young may try to flee the country and had ordered that his passport be seized. He was then threatened with jail unless he could account for his missing millions. Meanwhile, it was said that Sir Tom Hunter had contributed towards the estimated £120,000 a year rent on the Regent's Park townhouse where Michelle and their two daughters were staying. Earlier it was thought he had also paid towards the girls' school fees. Young still maintained that he was penniless and applied for legal aid, though lawyers continued to work for him for the time being for free.

Michelle doubted his claims of poverty after a phone call he had made to their daughters.

'Last week, he told Scarlet he would buy her a Rolls-Royce Phantom for her seventeenth birthday,' she told the *Mail on Sunday*. 'He said he was on the verge of a deal involving Bill Clinton that would make him one of the richest men in the world. He also said he wanted Scarlet to be friends with Philip Green's daughter Chloe. He told her that Philip would take the girls around Topshop and let Scarlet have anything she wanted. Thankfully, she doesn't want to take up the offer.'

Just the previous month, the rent payments had stopped and she faced eviction.

Back in court, Mrs Young was claiming maintenance, pending her claim for up to half his assets. Her barrister, Christian Kenny, insisted that, as Young had failed to answer questions about his assets, he was now in contempt of court. But Young's barrister, Philip Perrins, said the husband was having difficulty getting documents because several properties had been repossessed. Young maintained that he was unable to pay creditors and could not even afford a lawyer to represent him. That was why he had had to apply for legal aid.

His wife claimed this was nonsense. She had obtained computer records showing that in 2006 he was worth £400 million. But by August 2007, Young claimed his property empire had collapsed and that he was so hard up he was insolvent with debts of over £27 million.

Clearly it was up to the judge to try and find out how much Young was then worth.

'There is a £400 million starting figure,' he said. 'I expect some documentation to show where it has all gone. There isn't any at the moment.'

Michelle Young was hot on the case. She had hired a team of former Scotland Yard detectives to investigate what has happened to the money. They were examining fresh documents and computer files in which Young had apparently stored details of his business dealings.

At another hearing a week later, Michelle's counsel, Richard Todd, QC, compared the case in the High Court in London to the plot of the 1985 Hollywood comedy *Brewster's Millions*. Mrs Justice Parker queried the reference to the film, adding: 'I know judges aren't supposed to say they are out of touch with popular culture.'

Inevitably, they are.

The QC explained that, in the film, Richard Pryor starred as a failing baseball player who was told that he will inherit $300 million if he can spend $30 million of it in thirty days and have nothing to show for it – only to discover how hard it is to get rid of so much money. Somehow, Mr Young had managed it.

Mr Todd said it was in August 2007 that Mr Young first claimed he was 'minus £27 million' and insolvent. Yet his wife had obtained information from computer hard drives that put his wealth at £400 million only the previous year.

'Where did it all go in such a short time?' Mr Todd asked.

Mr Todd also asked how it was that, as recently as 15 May 2009, Mr Young had been represented by Geoffrey Cox, QC, a leading financial lawyer, if he had no money. Cox's time certainly did not come cheap. He earned £1 million as part of the defence team in the Jubilee Line fraud trial that collapsed in 2005 after almost two years at the Old Bailey.

Similarly, Mr Todd wondered how it was that, 'with apparently no visible means of support', Young had been flying back and forth between the UK and Germany, where his main working base was then located.

Mr Young had also failed to answer the financial questionnaire sent to him a year before. He had been required to do so under court order and was therefore in contempt of court.

The barrister told Mrs Justice Parker that Mrs Young had been served with notice to quit her Regent's Park home, and her daughters faced the prospect of having to leave their expensive fee-paying school. For the first two years of the divorce, her husband had seen to it that the £10,000-a-month rent on the property and the girls' £36,000-a-year private school fees had been paid – though, again, there are suggestions he had been helped by his friend, Sir Tom Hunter.

Mrs Young was pleading poverty.

'It's not about losing the luxury lifestyle – the houses, the jets, the jewels, the cars – my daughters and I can live without it,' said Michelle. 'I brought them up with their feet on the ground, despite the lifestyle we had. It's about not knowing where we will be living six months or a year from now or what school my daughters will attend. It's living every day and night knowing that our lives are hanging by a thread.'

The judge said that Mr Young had had plenty of time to provide the financial details he had been asked for and agreed that he was now in contempt of court. She gave him three months to come up with the information required. The deadline was set at 7 September 2009. If, at a further hearing on 28 September, he had failed to comply with the order he would go to jail for six months.

And when the deadline for producing the papers ran out, Mrs Young's lawyer was insistent that Mr Young should 'hear the clang of prison gates'.

'Mrs Young has no wish to see the father of her children

committed to prison,' he said, 'but the fact is, he is a man who quite plainly has no regard to his duties to her or to the court to provide the necessary information. This husband ought to hear the clang of the prison gates. The effect of prison can alter behaviour once it has been sampled. He ought to know what it is like if he doesn't comply with court orders.'

The barrister said Mr Young's attempts to assure the court he intended to comply were 'mere platitudes' and his apparent contrition was 'cynically contrived'. Without Scot Young's co-operation, finding out how much he was worth or where the money had gone may well prove impossible.

The detective leading the investigation said that they were looking into, not just Mr Young's business dealings, but also those around him.

'This is an extremely complex case which has been frustrated by Mr Young's failure to provide the information, as has been requested numerous times, and was borne out by Justice Parker's comments this week,' said the investigator. 'Progress is being made not only into Mr Young's affairs, but into the affairs of those who may have been intrinsically involved in his business activities. We're confident we will find the assets which Mrs Young alleges he and his associates have secreted.'

The judge also ordered Mr Young to pay his wife's legal costs on an 'indemnity' basis – that is, the highest scale of court costs – despite his insistence he had no money to pay. Young was then representing himself in court because his legal aid had been stopped, though Richard Caring of The Ivy soon stepped in with a loan of £50,000 to cover his legal expenses. Caring was thought to be worth £350 million.

He told the *Daily Telegraph* why he was helping Young out.

'He's not a bad guy and I think that he's being vilified,' Caring said. 'I have known him for many years and he came to see me. If you can help out, that is what old friends do. I have lent him £50,000. It's for whatever he wants to use it for, whether it is legal fees or anything.'

Young asked the court for further chance to answer the outstanding questions about his finances.

'I can give a narrative report of my financial collapse between 2004 and 2006,' he said, but he was told written records were required.

There were other problems. Young said his attempts to get to grips with this complex task, at a time when he had no legal advisers, had resulted in mental health problems that landed him in hospital.

As the case dragged on, the judge heard argument over whether she should extend the suspension of the six-month jail order, which was imposed for Mr Young's contempt of court, to give him more time to comply. Young continued to insist that, after his property empire collapsed he was being pursued for £27 million by creditors and expected to be made bankrupt.

David Balcombe, QC, another barrister now representing Mrs Young, was sceptical.

'This is a man who has enjoyed a massive fortune and now says it is all gone,' he said, 'but is unable to provide any worthwhile information why it has all gone and where it has all gone.'

Even though he said he had nothing, Mr Young's assets had been subjected to a freezing order up to £60 million. He was allowed £6,000 a week towards his living expenses as well as a reasonable sum for legal expenses. However, he maintained that this was money he did not have.

Mr Young's mental state now became key to the case. The court was told that Mr Young had only recently been released from hospital after being detained for two weeks under the

Mental Health Act after the stress of the case had caused him to suffer a breakdown. He had spent a week in an NHS North London hospital with an unspecified psychiatric disorder and was still being treated as an outpatient.

Philip Marshall, a counsel provided by Richard Caring, said: 'He suggested the fact that it was an NHS hospital showed it was a genuine breakdown. I could see him knocking on the door of the Priory, but finding himself restricted to the level of constraint that he was, it would be an altogether surprising method for him to adopt. It is the total antithesis of what his wife suggests he continues to enjoy in terms of wealth and affluence.'

David Balcombe questioned this. He said the hospital had provided very little detail about Mr Young's illness.

'It may seem unkind on Mrs Young's part to have misgivings, but if the symptoms which Mr Young is meant to have manifested at the end of August were feigned, he wouldn't be the first to have adopted that ruse,' he said. 'We cannot say whether it was genuine or nothing more than a ploy.'

Nevertheless, Philip Marshall that Mr Young had done his best.

'He started to assemble such documents as he had,' Marshall said. 'That was interrupted by a process where he increasingly became unable to focus on what he was required to do. Ultimately by 28 August this year, he was admitted to hospital.'

Mr Young, Marshall went on, was under enormous pressure and would have had to have pulled off the 'most dramatic scam' to fake his illness. Besides, Mr Young had not been ungenerous. He had paid his wife £1.2 million since the pair separated and she now wanted £48,000 a month in maintenance.

Though the figure sounded huge, Balcombe explained that it was not excessive.

'The sort of lifestyle which may be enjoyed by the very privileged few does in fact cost a great deal to support,' he said.

The battle between the couple was now joined on another front. Mrs Young had been served a possession order on the £2.8 million apartment. But her lawyers alleged that there was more to her impending eviction than meets the eye. The owners of the property were listed on the land registry as the Bollands, a wealthy couple from New York, but Mrs Young claimed the home was actually owned by her ex-husband.

Mr Balcombe said: 'There were some misgivings as to who was behind that notice to quit. It is believed on the wife's side that the ultimate owner is not the person named as the landlord but Mr Young himself and that he has been using this as another means of increasing pressure.'

Mrs Justice Parker then granted Young a ten-week extension, conceding that activating the suspended sentence should be put off until 13 November so that independent psychiatrists could examine Mr Young. She gave him until 9 November to produce documentation detailing his financial position. He would then face six months in jail if he failed to produce the information requested about his financial state and business affairs, plus UK bank accounts and tax records.

These court battles were now taking place in full glare of the media. Michelle's solicitor, Ayesha Vardag, issued a press statement, saying: 'Michelle Young has no desire to see her husband go to prison. She simply wants him to provide the court with the information it has ordered of him so that their case may be conducted properly and fairly.'

Mrs Young also told the press: 'I am shocked that my husband is still claiming he has lost his fortune. The judge has spared him the sanction of jail for now, but I am delighted that he has been placed on a very short timetable to provide the court with the information we need. The judge's order will at last reveal the whereabouts of my husband's fortune, which included expensive homes, cars, jewellery and yachts.'

Michelle went on to tell the *Daily Mail*: 'It is bewildering for the girls. He asked one of them last week to come to live with him in his new luxury apartment, which doesn't exactly chime with the idea that he has lost everything. In truth, we simply don't know how he has been living for the past three years.'

She also condemned the friends who had been helping him out.

'This is a man who rubs shoulders on equal terms with some of the richest and most famous men in Britain,' she said. 'I cannot believe they support his current behaviour towards his family.'

Michelle also had a message for her husband.

'I want Scot to know that I am not going to roll over,' she said. 'I mean business.'

Plainly, she was up against an operator. A friend said: 'His actions have made it difficult for her to fight for what she believes is rightfully hers. It looks as though the ruthlessness he has shown in his business life is now being brought to bear upon his family.'

But in this clash of the titans, Michelle would give as good as she got. Determined to get to the bottom of where the money had gone, she amassed a formidable team of experts, managed by financial consultants Temple Regulatory Service Limited. This was costing a great deal of money, so she was attempting to strike a third party litigation funding deal with them. While not exactly a 'no win, no fee' agreement, she was hoping they would pay some of the legal fees in exchange for a share in any money they might win. Besides, the company was optimistic.

A spokesman for Temple admitted that it was a complex case.

'Mr Young missed the court deadline to provide the required financial papers and is now in contempt of court.' But they were 'confident of achieving a resolution soon'.

In the end, Mrs Young found additional funding elsewhere. She signed a deal with Mayfair-based Harbour Litigation Funding, who usually provide funding for commercial law suits. This was their first foray into the divorce market. Before the financial crisis, private banks were eager to provide loans to help cash-strapped divorcees pay their legal fees in the hope of securing their business long-term. But as the value of assets dipped, it became much more difficult for stay-at-home wives, in particular, to find funding in divorce cases. Banks have also become reluctant to step in as British courts have thrown up a series of unpredictable rulings in big-money cases and banks feel they may be running too much in terms of risk as the outcome of some of these cases is uncertain.

But Harbour was hard-headed in its attitude.

'Collectively, the Harbour team has funded sixty-six commercial cases,' said Susan Dunn, Harbour's head of litigation funding. 'While the Young case is a divorce matter, in truth it has the same elements as a commercial dispute, and as such it fits with the core business that we undertake.'

In return, finance companies require twenty or thirty per cent of the final payout. It was worth the risk. London had become the divorce capital of the world in the wake of settlements such as the record £48 million awarded to the former wife of insurance tycoon John Charman in 2006.

CHAPTER 5

THE PENNILESS TYCOON

Despite the courtroom reverses, Scot Young was still upbeat.

A friend of Mr Young said that the tycoon was 'very positive about reaching an out-of-court settlement with Michelle. He intends to provide for his wife and children and is furious he has been portrayed as a bad husband and father.'

Asked if, in that case, Mr Young was not penniless, the friend said: 'No comment. He is a private man and his financial affairs will forever remain his business.'

All he would say was that Mr Young had amassed his fortune through 'property transactions, high-tech investments and telecom investments' and that he had been living in America for the three years, before returning to London.

Young issued a statement of his own, denying that he owned the property occupied by his ex-wife and saying: 'I have done everything to assist in every way to assure my family has occupation of the property.'

Michelle Young was adamant though. A friend, who asked not to be named, told *The Times* that the owners of the property sent a letter to all of Mrs Young's neighbours informing them that she was to be evicted.

'She's already fighting one court battle over the divorce, now she has to appear in the county court for this,' said the anonymous friend. 'The toll this is taking is tremendous. It's amazing a father would allow his own children to be forced out of their home. Michelle has no idea what she will do if this goes ahead. She may even squat.'

Another friend said: 'At the end of the day, it's a tragedy. It's a story of how money can't buy you happiness – in fact, completely the reverse. This case, with so much money at stake, has permanently damaged them as human beings.'

Despite her new source of funding, Mrs Young lost her court battle to stay on in her luxury home, even though she claimed that being evicted from the property would cause her and her two daughters 'exceptional hardship'. At the County Court in London on 14 October 2006, Felix Geiringer, representing New Yorkers Peter and Charlotte Bolland – the legal owners of the house in Regent's Park Terrace, North London – seized the opportunity to launch an extraordinary attack on Mrs Young. He accused her of being unable to adjust to life without access to extraordinary wealth.

Mr Geiringer said that, despite her reduced circumstances, she 'persisted' in wanting to live in a luxurious home, have her children educated at one of the most expensive schools in London and dressing in the most expensive clothes – even though she no longer had the money to support such a lifestyle.

'The fact that she continues to wish to live in an £8,666-a-month house, to school her children in an expensive school, to come to court dressed in very fine clothes – the fact that she makes these choices does not bring her within the realm of exceptional hardship,' he said. 'Nobody in this country needs to be homeless. If she's being evicted then the local council has an obligation to provide her with housing. She has access to benefits, her children can be schooled for free. The fact is that she is not seeking benefits that are available to her.'

The Bollands were petitioning for possession of the property on the grounds of non-payment of rent. The court was told that about £24,222 was owed to the landlords and this was rising by £284.93 a day.

Speaking for Mrs Young, Claire Van Overdijk said the defendant had sold all her jewellery to support herself and her daughters, seventeen-year-old Scarlet and Sasha, fifteen.

'In order to be able to survive and support her two daughters... she has sold all her jewellery now and has no assets worth selling to her name,' she said. 'Mrs Young's funds are effectively zero. At this moment in time she has no funds to her name.'

Mrs Van Overdijk said the defendant further owed £36,000 to her daughters' private school and £120,000 to a former solicitor. Mrs Young told Central London County Court that her husband said he'd paid the £8,656-a-month rent until December. But the court heard no such agreement was in place for the Regent's Park property. Geiringer said Mrs Young was offered the chance to take over paying the £8,656 monthly rent from 23 July, but had not paid, despite remaining in the property.

'On a cold-hearted, rational assessment of her own evidence, the defendant is failing to come to terms with a change in her personal circumstances,' said Mr Geiringer. 'One can be sympathetic to that, and can accept that she is having a very hard time, but in my submission that does not reach the level of exceptional hardship. The circumstances the defendant finds herself in are not more difficult than the average person facing eviction. Everybody who is evicted from their residence has difficulties associated with that eviction.'

Mrs Young accused her husband of betraying her and his two daughters. She insisted that the property was actually owned by her husband and the Bollands were simply acting as his nominees.

The defence asked whether the matter could be dealt with in the High Court where Mr Young was due to appear before Mrs Justice Parker on 13 November to disclose evidence of his assets. The application was refused.

District Judge Michael Gilchrist said he did not believe the ownership dispute affected the county court's ability to deal with the case. Mrs Young said she could not remember if she had signed an agreement allowing the landlord to give her sixty days' notice to leave. Mr Gilchrist said he could only assume that it had been signed and he agreed a possession order, ruling that she would have to leave the property within six weeks. Initially she had been told that she would have to leave in four weeks, but her lawyer successfully argued that she needed longer to make arrangements. The judge told her to 'get used to being poor'.

When told of the eviction, Michelle said: 'My husband, Scot Young, has totally abandoned his responsibilities to his young daughters, and his failure to provide a safe and secure home for them is causing exceptional emotional torment. He appears to have no concern for the welfare of his girls, let alone me. He and those who aid him should be ashamed. He is clearly trying to destroy me and break our resolve to fight for what is rightfully ours. Allowing his family to end up on the street is a despicable act and people will start to see what sort of a man he is.'

She also issued a statement saying that she was considering an appeal.

A close friend of Mrs Young said: 'She's already fighting one court battle over the divorce. It's amazing a father would allow his own children to be forced out of their home… The toll this is taking is tremendous. Michelle has no idea what she will do.'

Scot Young did not attend the court and complained to the *Daily Express* that he was unfairly being portrayed as the villain and strenuously denied his wife's claims that he owned the Regent's Park property. Her allegation, he said, was 'absolute rubbish'. He insisted he paid the rent a year in advance, but the estate agency he paid has gone under.

'His main concern is for his daughters and making sure they are looked after and safe and happy,' said a friend. 'It is ludicrous to suggest he would see them or Michelle homeless. It is terrible luck that the estate agents have gone bust and taken a year's rent money with them – but Scot intends to pay the rent and the girls' school fees. He wants more than anything to rebuild his relationship with his girls.'

Young himself said: 'These are private and confidential family matters. I have done everything I can to assist my family's continued occupation of the property. Michelle knows this. I have nothing further to say.'

It has to be said life in London is different to the rest of the country. For the super-rich – or even for the apparently suddenly poor like the Youngs – the figures are staggering. So, with the multi-million-pound divorce now in the headlines, the *Dundee Courier* went to interview Scot Young's 'ain folk' in Clepington Street.

One-time neighbour Daniel Irvine said: 'It is good that he has done so well with his life and has become so wealthy, but it's odd that he's saying he has lost it all.'

That puzzled everyone, including his wife. But the real question was: had he lost it all? Another resident named Gary Logan had drawn inspiration from Young's meteoric rise.

'It just shows how close knit the world is,' he said. 'I'm astonished that someone from this backyard has risen so far.'

He had risen, only to fall again. Paul Bowers, who ran a garage in Clepington Street, was hoping for some work on Young's collection of classic cars.

'This is a humble area now,' he said, 'and that's quite a story that that chap in the news came from that block across the road. We don't get many people coming in here with Bentleys and the like, but I'll keep my eye out for him.'

Lorraine McLeod lived in a flat at 8 Clepington Street before moving to a bigger flat in Broughty Ferry in 2011. She said she was shocked to learn that a former resident of the block was the infant Scot Young.

'I've been reading about that case in the papers and it said he was from Dundee, but I'd never have guessed he was from this tenement block,' she said.

The area, she thought, had changed.

'He would have been too young to know anything about this area at the time and I don't know if he knew it too well when he grew up a bit,' she said, 'but I don't suppose he would think much of this area now. There are lots of problems with youngsters playing in the back gardens and damaging fences. It's a far cry from the life that Scot Young grew into.'

Whatever his background, Scot Young knew that he had to make some semblance of compliance with the orders of the High Court. With the trial now being held, to all intents and purposes, in public, too many people were asking what he had to hide. Not the least of them was Michelle, who voiced her concerns in the newspapers.

'If he really has lost all of his money, why would he risk going to prison just to keep the details of those deals a secret?' said Michelle. 'What does he have to hide? What or who is he trying to protect?'

So when what was fast becoming the most expensive divorce case on record returned to the High Court on 13 November 2009, the threat of him being sent to jail was immediately lifted. Although he had missed the 9 November deadline for delivery of documents, the following day, he had provided thousands of pages of financial information to his wife's lawyers.

While Young now claimed that this satisfied the court order that he should disclose where the money has gone, the defence team were far from satisfied.

'Just two days before we were due back in court, fifty lever-arch files were delivered to my team. We hadn't had time to read them, so the case was adjourned again,' said Michelle.

'We have not yet made a full assessment of the quality of his disclosure and how helpful it will be in establishing where his wealth has gone,' said David Balcombe QC, again acting for Mrs Young. 'However we have come to the firm conclusion that his disclosure has not been full and frank and not in accordance with the court's expectations.'

Young gave no explanation why it had taken him so long to comply with a disclosure order made more than a year before. There were 'severe misgivings about his veracity,' her barrister said. At future hearings, the court would have to assess 'the scale of his duplicity'.

However, the court was told that Young had 'made further financial provision' for his wife Michelle pending their divorce. The money was thought to have come from third parties, as Young claimed to have lost a further £1.6 million since June.

Mr Justice Bennett agreed that the threat of prison for failing to disclose details of his finances would continue to hang over Mr Young's head until the information he had supplied was assessed. He still had to answer a questionnaire setting out alleged deficiencies in information provided so far and must to do now. His passport would remain impounded by the High Court Tipstaff. The case was adjourned until 17 December 2006. Even then, it was thought that Young would be able to put off being questioned about his financial position until the following year.

Michelle claimed that her husband's delaying tactics were taking their toll.

'It has been emotional torture,' she told the *Daily Telegraph*. 'The case has been going on so long and he has come up with so many excuses. It keeps being adjourned.'

By then the case had been going on for two-and-a-half years, but she was determined to get justice and be given her due.

'We started off with nothing,' she said. 'It is not fair that I am being portrayed as this gold-digger. I put up with him for nearly twenty years. I am convinced he is keeping the money in off-shore accounts so it looks like he is broke.'

While it was easy for paper investments to go up in smoke, it was harder to make real estate disappear. Prior to their separation, Mr Young owned a string of properties in Mayfair and Knightsbridge worth at least £32 million. Mrs Young was puzzled. Somehow, since then, Mr Young has lost all of these assets and ended up with a balance of less than zero. It was not possible to say whether he sold them or gave them away, because he had produced no receipts, deeds or papers to illustrate the deals he made. By the time the case was back in court again, Mr Young had provided another fourteen boxes of files.

In the meantime, she had to endure 'hardship'. In mid-

November, she moved from the townhouse in Regent's Park to a smaller property in St John's Wood. But there was still the matter of the outstanding £36,000 in school fees. Her daughters, Scarlet, who was studying for her A-levels, and Sasha, who was working towards her GCSEs, had two weeks left at school before they would be turned away.

On top of the pressure of the exams and the disruption of their schooling, they had been deeply troubled by the bitter battle between their parents.

'They do not want to talk to their father at the moment,' said Michelle.

When the Youngs returned to court on 17 December, Scot claimed that his situation had declined even further. He was getting by on £150 a week 'pocket money' provided by a friend named James Creed, a sixty-four-year-old business-man from Ealing, West London. Nevertheless, Mrs Young asked the judge to order him to pay her £35,000 a month – slashing £13,000 from her previous demand for £48,000 a month – until there was a full hearing to decide what share of his assets she should have. Again she faced losing her home and becoming destitute. She was, she said, down to her last £30,000.

'About a year ago, I sold off all of my Graff jewellery and the antiques I had, as we had nothing else to live on,' she told the newspapers. 'I got barely twenty per cent of the value of £1-million worth of jewels. But with school fees and legal bills to pay, that money didn't last long.'

An initial assessment of the records Mr Young had provided showed that the two houses they owned in London's Belgravia, a university hall of residence in Lincoln and their mansion in Miami were worth more than £116 million in total, although their value was reduced to £87 million by borrowings Mr Young made against them. Mr Balcombe also said Mr Young appeared to have had investments and shares in various companies, including O$_2$ and firms called Dione and Kiosks.

Nevertheless Young maintained that all this money had disappeared and that he was so short of funds he no longer had a bank account. His barrister, Philip Marshall QC, said Mrs Young's legal team had failed to find evidence of any income or asset he could draw on to pay maintenance. But Mr Balcombe said there were 'numerous discrepancies and deficiencies' between what Mr Young had told banks about the extent of his wealth and what he had told the court. Since the couple split in 2006, Mrs Young had received more than £1 million in living and housing expenses and she insisted that, rather than coming from rich benefactors, all this money actually belonged to him.

'We say it is stretching credulity to say while all this money has been made available, that the husband has been getting by on a weekly allowance, his pocket money, of £150 a week. It's simply incredible,' said Mr Young's barrister, David Balcombe. What's more, the tycoon had also been seen 'wining and dining' at expensive London establishments, while still pleading poverty.

'If he really is on his uppers, if he is scrounging around on his pocket money of £150 a week, why hasn't he gone out and got himself a job?' Mr Balcombe said.

Mrs Justice Black plainly did not believe that Mr Young had lost all his money. However, for the moment she would make an interim ruling. This would be 'a sticking plaster' in advance of a full divorce hearing the following year, she said, and she ordered the supposedly penniless property tycoon to pay his wife £27,500 a month for maintenance and legal fees.

In her ruling, the judge acknowledged that the family had historically lived a luxurious lifestyle and that £27,500 a month would be seen by some as 'exceptionally generous'.

'It's not nearly as much as the wife would say she required, but it's intended to be on top of rent and school fees,' she said. Strangely for a man who claimed to be living on pocket money, Young had already agreed to pay £6,500 a month rent and school fees of £36,000 a year on top of this.

While this was not nearly as much as Michelle would have wanted, the judge said she had to 'have regard to the reality of the situation'. Even so, this was the highest maintenance order in the country and would keep the family in the 'lifestyle to which they had become accustomed'.

Phillip Marshall, for Mr Young, said the wife's legal team had spent £400,000 in three months attempting to prove that the tycoon had hidden vast sums from the courts, but they had been unable to identify any hidden income or assets. It was she, not he, who should be looking for a job, he said.

'The sums sought by the wife are wholly disproportionate to anything that's remotely affordable, even assuming my client had the wealth which the wife asserts he had,' Philip Marshall said.

Mrs Justice Black was unsympathetic though.

'The couple have historically lived a luxurious lifestyle on money made by the husband in the course of his activities as an entrepreneur and property dealer which enabled him to accumulate many millions of pounds,' said the judge. 'Looking at the case as a whole I am entirely satisfied that the husband has available monies to pay maintenance.'

Mr Balcombe was still insistent that Mr Young had put his worth at more than £120 million in letters drawn up by his solicitors. But the judge said this did not mean that Mr Young had 'hard cash'. There were assets and other ways he could find the money.

'The reality is funds and benefits in kind have been made available to this family on a large scale despite the husband saying he has no means,' she said.

Mr Young protested that this was not the case. The £1.2 million his wife had received over the past three years had been provided by wealthy friends, but they could not be relied on to continue such grants. He had already borrowed money to pay off arrears of the daughters' school fees and to secure payments for the next three months.

But his arguments did not wash with Mrs Justice Black. She said that 'significant questions remain about the accuracy of the husband's disclosure to the court', while some of the data he provided was 'so uninformative as to be virtually useless... Matters had been identified which make one cautious about the reliability of the husband's ability or inability to pay. Luckily I'm not confined to what he says and can take my own critical look at what may be the situation.'

Mr Young had made many millions from his entrepreneurial activities and received hand-outs from his wealthy friends which went 'beyond mere generosity,' the judge said. However, in property alone, Mr Young appeared to be worth £87 million. Other assets brought that figure up to £124 million.

'I am entirely satisfied that the husband has available monies to pay maintenance,' she said. However, she was nothing if not evenhanded. She said that she found some aspects of the case came direct from *Alice in Wonderland* – for example, at one stage, Mrs Young claiming £12,675 a month to cover sports and hobbies.

Even though she would have to cut back on her leisure activities, after the ruling, Mrs Young said: 'I am relieved because this has been torture and tormented me and my children. We have to wait and see if he pays it now. I have said before that £400 million is just the tip of the iceberg and I stick to that. We have to wait and see if he pays it now but if he doesn't he will be in serious trouble because the penal notice will go back on him. After not having any maintenance for eighteen months at this stage I am relieved. The sum is coming so that me and my children will be able to sleep better. My daughters and I are not looking for pity. We are looking for justice.'

Mrs Justice Black also ruled that because of his 'unreasonable conduct' in failing to provide full disclosure of his assets, Mr Young would have to pay £600,000 towards his wife's legal bills. Afterwards Mr Young said: 'I didn't have anywhere near the kind of wealth she says I had. Yes, we lived lavishly, but I ended up over-extending myself.'

A source close to the businessman was adamant that Scot Young was pot-less.

'This is all bullshit,' he said, 'Everybody knows there was no £400 million. I don't know why everybody is so obsessed with this bloke. If anybody finds any money they should print the fucking map.'

So Mr Young was penniless, but perhaps only comparatively so.

CHAPTER 6

FRIENDS IN HIGH PLACES

As the high-powered divorce case entered its fourth year, the court decided to look into the group of Young's friends who had secretly paid Michelle over £1.2 million to keep her head above water. The judge said these payments were 'exceptionally generous'. The enquiries unsettled her benefactors who wanted to keep their generosity out of the public eye.

Documents presented to the court revealed that Sir Tom Hunter had paid Michelle £124,000 in the form of rent and school fees for the two children.

'He wanted to help the family because he saw no reason why the girls should suffer at a time of need,' said a spokesman for Hunter.

Arcadia boss Sir Philip Green, the documents said, had given £110,000 to the Youngs for rent on the town house in Regent's Park, as well as £5,000 of Topshop vouchers for Scarlet and Sasha. But Green, whose Arcadia group owns Topshop and BHS, was adamant that he had not given Michelle money directly.

'I never paid her a penny,' he said, adding that he had not had many dealings with Scot Young recently and that he did not want to comment further.

His office later admitted that there had been two payments totalling £80,000 to Michelle Young's estate agents to cover the rent. It also said Green may have given 'about £1,000 to one of the daughters as a Christmas present'.

Harold Tillman, the chairman of Jaeger and Aquascutum, was also surprised to hear claims in the court papers that he had given £92,000 to Michelle Young. His office told *The Sunday Times*: 'He says that he knows of Scot Young but does not know him well and has had no financial involvement with him whatsoever and therefore cannot really help in this case.'

Later, Tillman attempted to clarify the statement, saying: 'I have in the past helped Scot Young who was at one time an acquaintance. I remember him coming to me for some help. But I have certainly not made any direct payment to his wife, although they may have had a joint bank account.'

According to the documents, other businessmen who had given the couple large sums included Stephen Kay, a Monaco-based film producer whose family ran a property empire in Manchester. Kay's son, Richard, paid £88,000 towards Scot Young's bill when he spent more than a year at the Ritz-Carlton hotel in Berlin. Andas mentioned earlier, restaurateur Richard Caring, who owns The Ivy, had lent Mr Young £50,000 towards legal fees.

In all, payments totalled more than £1.3 million, with the bulk – £1,175,000 – going to Michelle. These payments began after the couple split in 2006. They now appeared have ceased

– to Michelle. Three months after the maintenance order had been made, her estranged husband had yet to pay the full £27,500 a month. She was particularly angry because it was through her father that he had got in touch with those who were now so generously helping him out. To put pressure on, she wanted details of their dealings.

'My father helped give Scot all these business contacts and he made hundreds of millions of pounds from this network,' she said. 'We will be asking him in court to give a full and frank disclosure of his finances, including details of third parties and institutions with whom he has had financial ties over the last twenty years.'

In response, Scot Young insisted that he had nothing to hide. His friends should be left out of it. Just because they were rich did not mean he was.

'The sums of money being mentioned in relation to my past wealth are totally absurd,' he said. 'I was never in that league. I believe I have complied with the judge's order on disclosure by delivering fifty-two lever arch files to my wife's solicitors and the court. As far as the payments to my wife are concerned, they were not secret and they were paid by friends to help a family who had fallen on hard times.'

Then the multi-million-pound divorce case took a sinister turn when Michelle said that she had called the police after a couple of attempted break-ins at her home in St John's Wood. She also claimed that computers at the firm of lawyers she had hired to represent her had been hacked into.

In April 2010, HM Revenue & Customs filed a bankruptcy petition against Mr Young for a little less than £2 million in unpaid taxes. So when the divorce case returned to the High Court over the non-payment of maintenance, Young told the judge: 'I believe this hearing is totally academic, I believe my affairs will now be in the hands of the trustee of the bankruptcy.'

Mrs Young was understandably furious.

'Bankruptcy is just another way for him to avoid paying any money,' she said.

Mrs Justice Black ruled that Mr Young would have to pay the costs of the last two maintenance hearings, amounting to £100,000 in all, on an indemnity basis. However she would not backdate the maintenance payments to July 2008 – shortly after Mr Young was said to have stopped paying.

The judge also noted that Mrs Young had claimed that her husband stopped making maintenance payments in 2008 after he found out that she had obtained information of his finances from the hard drive of a computer.

'The husband denies that and says he does not have sufficient finances,' noted Mrs Justice Black, 'and that he was insolvent in December 2009 and is now bankrupt.'

By then Mrs Young's situation had got worse. Her savings had been reduced to £13,000 and she had run up huge debts with solicitors now said to be in excess of £660,000. The judge said Mrs Young's solicitors would 'have to consider their position'. Meanwhile Mrs Young's lawyer said her client was facing the prospect of losing her home again, schooling for her children and legal representation.

'Scarlet, who is taking her A-Levels, isn't sleeping and is finding it very difficult to cope with the stress of exams and the risk of being made homeless,' said Sarah Phipps, representing Mrs Young. 'The husband has not paid any maintenance since April 2008 and the school fees are £23,000 in arrears and the girls' schooling is obviously in jeopardy.'

Mr Young should pay maintenance of £500,000 – back to July 2008 – and his ex-wife's legal costs, her lawyer insisted.

Mr Young, who represented himself in court, 'felt it appropriate to say very little,' Mrs Justice Black said. 'His submission is academic – he has been made bankrupt.' He could hardly be expected to pay the £27,500 a month she had ordered when he was bankrupt. It was only the generosity of wealthy benefactors who provided him with an average of £400,000 a year since 2006 that had kept him afloat.

However, there was a new string to Mr Young's bow. A bankruptcy trustee would be appointed to clear up her husband's financial affairs. The judge said Mrs Young's legal team should now consider the effect of the bankruptcy on the divorce proceedings and whether they should 'permit the trustee in bankruptcy to investigate the husband's circumstances rather than proceeding to incur further costs by doing so themselves'.

On the other hand, there was more bad news. The full divorce proceedings, still a month away, were threatened by Mr Young's failure to make all of the scheduled maintenance payments, Mrs Justice Black said. It was clear now that the Youngs' two daughters would have to leave their fee-paying school.

'The worry isn't that they might have to attend a state school instead of a private school,' said Michelle. 'It's that they don't want to leave the school they're in at this crucial time. The girls are in the middle of their GCSEs and A-levels. They don't want to leave their friends.'

Michelle insisted she cannot work because she has more than a full-time job running the extraordinarily complex investigation into her husband's missing millions. What's more, they were going to have to move again.

'I don't like to admit it to myself because I like to stay strong, but the prospect of a council house is becoming very real,' she said. 'It's in the back of my mind all the time...

When I think of the places we used to call home, I can't believe we find ourselves here. That old life feels like a distant dream.'

She told the court that eviction from her new home would cause her 'extreme hardship'. Her appeal was met with derision from her landlords' solicitor, who told her that, until she was living on benefits in a council house, she could not claim to know what hardship was.

'I found the lawyer really hostile,' she said. 'It could have been my husband himself speaking.'

Despite having Harbour Litigation Funding behind her, she still found the situation hard to cope with.

'There have been times – plenty of them – when we have felt like we can't keep fighting,' she said. 'It hasn't stopped him applying pressure day after day in the hope that we will crack. I find it hard to accept that the man I married – even though he is like a total stranger to me now – would want to destroy me in this way.'

But she was not fighting for herself alone.

'It is even more upsetting to think that he could do this to his own daughters,' she said. 'We cried and cried when the court served the eviction, but I told the girls: "Don't worry. I will work hard and I will make sure that we get what we're due." I have to believe that.'

On the other side, Scot Young said he felt that the bankruptcy had vindicated his claims to have been penniless. Now his financial affairs would be in the hands of a bankruptcy trustee with whom he would be happy to co-operate.

'I have battled for some years and hopefully this will bring closure and allow me to move on,' he said. 'I have every intention of looking after the children and my wife to the best degree I can. She must allow me to get back into the business arena and stop the media circus surrounding the case, which is damaging to my children.'

He said he wanted more than anything to rebuild his relationship with his daughters, though Michelle claimed that the girls had chosen not to speak to him at all. Scot's friends complained that he was 'sick and tired of his wife's attempts to portray him as a bad father'.

Some of the newspapers were now gleefully pointing out that Michelle Young might end up with nothing. But she was determined that his bankruptcy was not going to be the end of it and would fight on for the sake of the girls.

She told the media: 'While "the fixer" to Russian oligarchs and British billionaires claims to be penniless he still has the means to retain some of Britain's finest legal representation. I'm doing this to make sure that my daughters and I won't have to worry for the future and at the same time this is a process to make history for an important case like this to receive public funding. This is twenty years of my life, this has had such a huge effect on me and my daughters. Like so many women, so many families in this situation, I want to stand up and make this change for justice.'

However, behind closed doors Harbour pulled out of their financial arrangement with Mrs Young, fearing that he really was broke.

'Previously, she has said that her husband is worth £400 million but she now says he is worth billions,' said a source close to the case. 'Harbour provided a bottomless pit of money to go chasing the assets she identified as belonging to him. If it had found them it would have taken a percentage of the settlement. But the fact Harbour has pulled out after three months says it all.'

A source close to Harbour said: 'It seems he was buying

CHAPTER 7

THE TAXMAN COMETH

Following her husband's bankruptcy, Michelle had a new weapon to hand when she threatened to present secret files on her estranged husband's dealings with the super-rich to the taxman. She said she would give HM Revenue & Customs a computer disk containing hundreds of pages of emails and other documents outlining his dealings in property, shares and film companies over the past five years.

The files had been held on the hard drive of a laptop used by the tycoon. He thought he had deleted them before handing the laptop over to his estranged wife for their daughters to use in the run-up to their exams. But she hired private detectives, including the former head of Scotland Yard's computer crime unit, to examine the laptop and recover a large amount of encrypted material.

But Scot was unfazed by the move.

'I have nothing to hide,' he said. 'A copy of the hard drive is with my former lawyers and I'm happy to give that to the Revenue.'

A source close to Mr Young told the *Daily Telegraph*: 'There is nothing secret about these files. They were on the hard drive of his computer.'

Young insisted that properties he had been linked to in a £100 million portfolio outlined on the hard drive had all been repossessed or sold. However, his wife's move caused further disquiet among his wealthy friends who had already told him privately they were unhappy with the publicity surrounding the case. For example, the files show that in 2004 he sold Berezovsky a London property at 27 Eaton Square estimated to be worth £4 million for just £350,000. But Young insisted that the price paid was the market value as the property had only a five-year lease. The computer disk and other documents contain details of transactions involving the sale of fifty properties, including half-a-dozen mansions in Belgravia, one of them the former home of Roman Abramovich.

The house at 28 Eaton Square, also valued at £4 million, was handed to a business associate in 2005 for £360,000, apparently in lieu of monies owed. Another prime property, 39 Chester Terrace, near Regent's Park in London, had been bought in 2002 for £2.75 million with a loan of £2.2 million. Mr Young sold it to a British Virgin Islands company, Balymena Equities, for £3.1 million in March 2007. This was after his supposed financial meltdown.

There were details of the deals he made for Wentworth Park in Surrey with its two hundred acres of grounds, containing several large cottages. Young purchased it for £16.8 million in 2000 and sold it to Berezovsky for £20.5 million the following year.

Then there was The Old Rectory at Wootton Place, bought for £6 million, sold for £9.5 million; the waterfront property at North Moorings Way, Coconut Grove, Miami, sold for £3.4 million; South Lodge in Knightsbridge, sold for £2.7 million; 111 and 112 Eaton Square, sold for £2.4 million; and 26 Belgrave Square, sold for £4 million. The *Daily Mail* also alleged that he owned 23 Wilton Crescent and 21 Upper Grosvenor Street – both sold for unknown figures – but Young denied it.

Court papers show that between 2004 and 2006, Young's portfolio was then estimated to be worth around £60 million. Some of this had already been salted away. One document from Murphy Salisbury, a firm of chartered accountants in Stratford-on-Avon, said that in March 2004 'Mr Young has a number of property investments, either in his own name, or companies that are beneficially owned by him.' At the time, it said, he was negotiating to release £40 million of his investments and his personal wealth was 'in excess of £100million'.

The files also contain references to film investments. Young discussed funding *Manolete* or *The Matador's Mistress*, a film about a Spanish bullfighter released in France in March 2010, starring Adrien Brody and Penelope Cruz. He confirmed he did invest in one film company because associates told him it would be 'tax-efficient'. Other files include references to a technology firm called EU Smart, which Sir Philip Green's wife Tina held some shares in.

Michelle Young was taking the drastic action of exposing this to the press and telling the taxman because, she said, she and her daughters faced penury as she was unable to pay school fees or rent due that week on their three-bedroom house in St John's Wood, London.

'I have been humiliated,' she said. 'He has stolen the last three years of our lives. We are just living one day at a time. He is eating in the finest restaurants with beautiful young models while my girls don't know their futures.'

Young said he had only one girlfriend at the time. She was twenty-eight-year-old American-born model Noelle Reno. That she should have her name linked to that of a pauper was something of a surprise. She was the former fiancée of Matthew Mellon, heir to the banking fortune and former husband of co-founder of Jimmy Choo, Tamara, who was also accessories editor of *Vogue*. He backed Noelle in the creation of the clothing brand Degrees of Freedom.

After they split in 2008, she sued him for £30 million, claiming that he had gone on crack cocaine binges, embezzled funds from the fashion business they had set up and started a campaign to 'belittle' her – even accusing her of embezzlement. At one stage, because of his 'repeated drug relapses', Noelle said she got Mellon to sign a contract to pay her $1 million if he fell off the wagon. The case was settled out of court.

Noelle was no stranger to the high life. She had groomed herself for success from an early age. Born into a conservative Catholic middle-class family in Seattle, her horizons soon extended beyond suburbia. As a child, she recalled: 'I was reading *Vogue* and I had a vision of where I wanted to be – it wasn't Seattle.'

At the age of thirteen, her girl-next-door pettiness landed a contact with the Elite modelling agency. This caused jealousy and alienated some of her schoolmates.

'Girls in high school were not very nice to me because of the modelling,' she said. 'I always wanted more true friendships.'

But there was more adolescent trauma to handle and she was just seventeen when her parents split up.

'So I know how to handle divorce,' she said.

Like the Young's split, the divorce was acrimonious. However, wounds heal and after fifteen years her parents were talking again.

Following the split, Noelle moved to Los Angeles with her mother. After starring in a Mercedes-Benz commercial, she was picked up by an acting agent and appeared in a couple of low-budget horror films. Then she met Matthew Mellon.

'We struck up a friendship,' she said. 'I came over to visit him in London and we ended up getting together.'

But there was more to their relationship than that.

'He was a bit of a Svengali with me – or he wanted to be,' she said. 'He said I would be great at running a fashion company. At the time Juicy Couture leisurewear was really popular in America, but none of the women I was friends with would wear it outside the house. So I saw a gap in the market for a more chic version in cashmere and silk.'

That was the birth of Degrees of Freedom. Then after four years the couple split up and, over her objections, he bought her out.

'I didn't want to sell,' she said. 'He had fifty-one per cent of the company and I had forty-nine,' she says. 'I had no idea, as a twenty-two-year-old, what signing that contract meant. Now I'm much wiser. But I'm glad. I sold to him just at the tip of the crisis, so I didn't have to ride the downturn.'

Following her settlement with Mellon, she went on to create the clothing line Z with Zandra Rhodes, though this failed to get off the ground. She also invested in a vintage jewellery company and described herself on her Twitter profile as 'fashion entrepreneur'.

Mellon went on to date designer Nicole Hanley, they would marry and have two children before starting a lifestyle brand. Meanwhile, Nicole returned briefly to the US. Her television career began when she became a presenter on Fashion TV, before moving on to be one of the hosts of *Ladies of London*.

She had originally met Scot Young in London when she was still with Mellon.

'It was in 2006 – June 21st or 22nd,' she said. 'Scot was driving around Belgrave Square and he pulled over to say hello to Matthew. And then we were introduced. There was definitely a spark.'

However, they did not hook up until the summer of 2009 when Young was already embroiled in his divorce case but, because of the family court reporting restrictions, it had yet to hit the headlines.

'They met in a West End eaterie and recognised one another because they'd been introduced through Matthew a few years ago,' said a friend that autumn. 'They started chatting and Scot asked her out on a date. They had a genuine connection and have been dating since June.'

But the strain of the divorce was already beginning to tell.

'Obviously it hasn't been the easiest time for Scot,' said the friend. 'He wants to get the divorce over as quickly as possible so that he can get on with his life with Noelle. She has been very supportive and has said she doesn't care that he is penniless.'

According to Noelle, it was three years to the day after they had been introduced in Belgrave Square that they met up again. She was having dinner with friends in the fashionable restaurant Cipriani when she spotted Scot dining with a mutual friend. By this time he had, apparently, lost all his money and had split from his wife.

'I went over to their table and Scot and I started a conversation,' said Noelle.

Young told her that the first news of his divorce was going to be in the papers the next day. But coincidence, Noelle's new fashion venture with designer Zandra Rhodes would be announced the following day too.

'So he said, "Let's get the papers and read them together tomorrow"' she said. That was their first date. From that day, they were rarely out of the press.

Young had already been parted from Michelle for two-and-a-half years and Noelle had no idea that their divorce would be a problem.

'Scot told me they would probably settle that summer,' she said. 'But it dragged on. I had no idea what it would turn into.'

With hindsight, she thought she should have walked away.

'It would have been wise for me to wait and let him figure out his divorce,' she said. 'But we would probably not have been able to do that. We were like magnets.'

Three months after they started dating, Scot proposed to her. But the couple were in no position to get married because of his on-going divorce. Some wondered what a young, loaded, supermodel would want with a balding, penniless former tycoon who was unable to ditch a rancorous ex-wife. Money was certainly not a factor in his attraction – as Noelle soon became all too painfully aware.

'Some people might have got the misconception that I am a gold-digger,' she said while house-hunting on *Ladies of London*. 'But look around, does this place say gold-digger to you?'

One place they saw in Marylebone, she said, 'smelled like her grandmother's house – not in a good way'. He said it was nice, but Noelle was firm.

'This is not the place for me,' she said. 'I deserve a bit better than this.'

Indeed, when it came to Young's riches, she knew she had missed her chance.

'Before I met Scot he was living this incredibly glamorous life with all sorts of Bentleys, mansions and jets,' she said. 'I met him at the wrong time.'

Certainly, their domestic surroundings were nowhere near as glamorous as those of the other chatelaines depicted in *Ladies of London*. But the couple's lifestyle was not cheap. Nevertheless there were ways they could make do.

'Scot has friends who continue to help him because he's made a lot of money for a lot of people over the years,' she said. 'I fund a lot. Scot has a ton of pride so it's been hard for him having me pay for things.'

Although he was brought up in relatively impoverished circumstances, he had to be domesticated.

'He started making money so young – promoting clubs when he was seventeen,' she said. 'I think he owned his first property at twenty-four. So his whole life he's had people making tea for him. When I first met Scot, he didn't know how to make a cup of tea. Now he's super-good at it.'

Although Noelle was happy to pick up the tab, the loss of his fortune had caused problems between them.

'I stopped letting him talk about it because it pissed me off,' she said. 'I mean, I'd have liked the Rolls, the Porsche and the estate – it's not fair!'

However, she was certain that Scot hadn't stashed the missing millions under the bed.

'I've not been living a lavish lifestyle for the past five years,' she said. 'And with all the forensic accountants that Michelle employed; all the private detectives she's had investigating us, if there was something she would have found it.'

Noelle, at least, was stoical about it. He had played the game and lost.

'Scot has always gambled in business,' she said. 'He's a big risk-taker, a big entrepreneur, he's very clever. But he took too many risks at one time, the project went bad and he was wiped out.'

Nevertheless, he never seemed short of a bob or two. An

acquaintance said: 'He never tried to hide what he had spent. He always had loads of cash with him. But he could also sometimes come across as shy.'

However, when it came to the missing millions, Noelle thought that Michelle was deluded.

'Scot was never worth the kind of money she talked about,' she said. 'She's got this idea that Scot is a super-genius who runs the world and that Philip Green is on his payroll.'

She insisted that it was Young's desire to keep the dealings of his wealthy friends and associates away from public scrutiny has meant he's been unable to prove his lack of funds.

'It's partly loyalty, and partly that he didn't keep all the records going back twenty years,' she said.

Even after five years of hardship and struggle, Noelle still planned to make a future with her man.

'We're planning on getting married next year and having kids very soon.' She said she would be happy to sign a prenup – though on his side it did not really seem necessary. 'I think everybody should. If you can't have that conversation with your partner then you shouldn't be getting married.'

While his prolonged battle in the divorce courts had made him wary of marriage, it had not dealt the possibly fatal blow. After all, in Noelle, he was getting someone who was both beautiful and generous.

'He would never, ever get married again if it wasn't for me,' she said. 'And he only wants to have a child because he wants to parent one with me – he thinks I'll be a great mum.'

She had no fears on that score.

'He's a fabulous father and his daughters adore him,' Noelle said. 'He sees them and has a good relationship with them. They've had a tough time but they've learnt to look after themselves.'

What's more she had faith in him. She was certain that there was light at the end of the tunnel and said that Scot was making big deals again. Noelle was sure that he would rebuild his fortune. Meanwhile he was supporting her in her career.

'Scot is a massive rock for me,' she said. 'I think I've become more successful and a much better person in business by having him in my life. We're best friends, and I've never met a man who's so selfless in supporting a woman... He is a closet feminist. He will support and champion me. Lots of guys won't do that.'

Her own business career was going from strength to strength. She was a partner in the accessories company Lulu's Estate Jewellery, doing the branding and marketing. And she was a brand ambassador for designer Carolina Herrera, the Mayfair private members' club Morton's, the Neville hair salon and Bentley cars.

'And there's another exciting project combining TV and retail, so watch this space!' she told *You* magazine.

Meanwhile, things were not going so well for the discarded wife. Once again, Michelle was looking for 'an angel investor' to help fund her case. The property developer Vincent Tchenguiz had reportedly shown interest but, at that point, had not committed any funds. However, Sofia Moussaoui, her solicitor, thought that it was better to leave the taxman to find out what had happened to her husband's assets as he had 'a bottomless pit in terms of resources'.

Young continued to maintain that he was 'delighted' that the taxman or the trustee in bankruptcy would be 'looking at this in a rational fashion, unlike my wife, who I believe is refusing to come to terms with the fact that we can no longer live a luxury lifestyle'.

HM Revenue & Customs appointed the accountants Grant

Thornton Partners to investigate his affairs and recover any assets. David Ingram from Grant Thornton quickly came to the conclusion that creditors were owed about £20 million.

'Clearly this is a case where there are differing versions of the truth,' he said. 'However, we have a great deal of experience in unpicking complex financial transactions to establish whether fraud or money laundering have taken place.'

CHAPTER 8

BATTLE OF THE BLONDES

This did not help Michelle Young who complained, again, that she felt 'humiliated' at having to apply for housing allowance from Westminster council. Her estranged husband's friends were no longer contributing towards Michelle's household budget.

'They don't like all the headlines,' said a friend. The money dried up and she had to apply for benefits.

'I have paid my taxes my whole life,' said Michelle. 'Now when I need help I have gone to the council. I am extremely grateful to them. I only need temporary help during these times of genuine need.'

Council housing officials told her that her application for support would be approved.

A spokeswoman for Westminster City council said: 'We cannot comment on individual claims. But as long as a household meets the eligibility criteria, they will be entitled to housing benefit rates set by the government based on the size of the accommodation they need.'

Mrs Young told them that she would repay the benefits when she received her divorce settlement, which she was still confident would run into millions. In the meantime, she would have to make do with a council flat not far from the three-bedroom house in St John's Wood she could no longer afford.

Meanwhile her estranged husband was living with friends in a £1 million apartment near Hyde Park and had been photographed dining in some of London's most expensive restaurants with girlfriend, Noelle Reno. Young insisted that she always paid the bill.

Two months later, they were living together in Lancaster Gate and were seen together at the Hennessy Gold Cup at Newbury.

'Scot is my best friend,' Noelle tells me. 'I just feel so comfortable with him.'

She said that Young was a dream housemate, while she was not always so easy to live with.

'I'm an insomniac, so I'm up four or five times in the night,' she admitted. 'If anyone is difficult to live with, then it's definitely me.'

But there was trouble in store for the doting couple. Reno was intending to visit her mother, a medical sales consultant, in Phoenix, Arizona, for Christmas but he would not be able to join them as his passport has been confiscated.

'I feel slightly torn because we were hoping Scot could join us, so he could meet my family, but they won't release his passport,' she told a gossip column. 'It's very sad because I don't want him to be on his own, but then I have to see my family. Christmas won't be the same without him.'

The couple were attending an Ella Krasner-hosted charity

event at the Electric cinema in Notting Hill, which was sponsored by Tod's. Wrangling to get his passport returned, Scot was condemned to a Christmas alone. It was all the more poignant because Christmas Day was Noelle's birthday.

'It's incredibly upsetting for Noelle as she hoped to be able to say goodbye to Scot before Christmas,' said a friend. 'Instead, the whole business is going to linger over the festive break.'

For Michelle and the girls, Christmas that year would be a modest affair. There would be no shopping at Harrods or dining at Le Manoir aux Quat' Saisons. Unlike previous years, there was no new Porsche to join the others in the drive on Christmas morning.

The situation was going from bad to worse. Not only was the £5,375-a-term Frances Holland School, one of the most distinguished girls' schools in the country, about to kick her two daughters out, they were threatening to start legal proceedings against Mrs Young for £32,000, the year's outstanding fees. If she could not pay, she would be made bankrupt, even though both parents were responsible for the fees.

Michelle believed that her husband was out to 'break' her while having fun in the sun with the nubile Ms Reno, who she dismissed as a 'small-time actress'.

In 2011, Michelle Young began a new offensive in the media, inviting Danae Brook of the *Daily Telegraph* to the small flat in Victoria she had been reduced to. No longer the elegant lady of the manor, Michelle padded around barefoot. To make room, she pushed aside heaps of legal papers as, for more than a year, she had played the role of unpaid lawyer, forensic accountant and detective. Ms Brook noted that Michelle had lost half-a-stone from anxiety and now served instant coffee.

'The scene is unrecognizable from the last time we met,' she wrote. 'A year ago, her pretty daughters were ushering me into a fabulously elegant Regency terrace house, arranged over four floors, with gilded mirrors and scented candles. The table we sat at was laid for dinner for at least twelve. It was the house of a very rich woman, a woman used to being very well looked after. Dividing her time between vast mansions in the English countryside and a waterfront house in Miami's South Beach, Ms Young had her hair coloured in London's top salons, wore only designer clothes and thought nothing of a manicure every other day. Now, her evenings are more likely to be spent with a pizza in front of the television.'

But Mrs Young had gained a new gravitas.

'These are not the things which matter to me,' she said. 'When you are fighting for your children's survival, it's not what you think about. I have been backed into a corner, so I am doing what any mother would do – fighting for a fair and just resolution.'

She complained that her husband was 'cruel, prone to extreme mood swings, a rich man who used money as a weapon'. His constant threat was to "make me homeless" if I left him.'

She still had nightmares about being homeless.

But it was her daughters that she was more worried about. The previous October, she had implored Young to turn up for Sasha's sixteenth birthday. Reluctantly, he agreed and, reflecting their reduced circumstances, they met in a small cafe.

'If he felt any guilt or remorse it didn't show,' said Michelle. 'Sasha asked if he'd take them to Mr Chow for a birthday meal, where we always used to go, and he said it would take him weeks to save up enough money for that. He just handed Sasha a wad of notes, wished her happy birthday, and left. He wouldn't tell us where he's living, and this was the first time we had seen him in months.'

There was worse to come.

'He called the girls one time and they could hear a woman giggling in the background,' Michelle said. 'They were so upset, I was up with them until three in the morning. They didn't want to speak to him any more after that.'

Pleas for him to stump up the school fees fell on deaf ears.

'When we saw him I begged him to at least pay the school fees,' she said. 'It is so cruel to cheat children of their future. Those girls have done so well, Scarlet had top results in all her subjects and Sasha is due to take ten GCSEs.'

Already they had been forced to move three times, which was incredibly disruptive for the girls and their education and the impasse of the school fees hung over them like the sword of Damocles.

'It has been unbearably unsettling, none of us knows where our things are – we've been living out of suitcases,' said Michelle. 'When the judge awarded me my maintenance order, we breathed a sigh of relief that day. I thought I had tasted my first breath of freedom. But since then he has not paid one penny. Where's the justice in that? Where are our human rights?'

Nevertheless, Michelle kept photographs of her marriage that she shed a tear over, though she did not often cry, she said. They showed happier times, full of smiles and hugs.

When Michelle and her girls look back at photographs of the life they used to have, it is not the houses, the jewels or the designer gowns that they miss the most.

'We miss being able to sleep at night,' said Michelle. 'This is like slow torture. There are days when I think: "How much longer can I go on?" But I have to pull myself together – for myself, for the girls and also for the fact that I am not the only woman in Britain who is going through this.'

She admitted that most women would find it hard to relate to the sums bandied about in her divorce. But she still felt that others could relate to her.

'I am not some woman who married a rich man,' she said. 'We had nothing when we started out. I devoted my life to him, I helped him build his business. Yet now I know he was manoeuvring behind my back to take it all away. He has taken the law into his own hands and manipulated the legal system. The pain of that kind of betrayal makes you numb. I find it hard to believe I ever loved him. Whatever I felt for him has died completely – and that goes for the girls, too. The mistake I made was to trust him to do right by me and by our daughters. It doesn't matter whether it's £400 million or £400, it is the principle that counts. That is what I am fighting for.'

But there was one thing she could rescue from the ruins.

'I will never regret my marriage because it produced two wonderful daughters,' she said. 'You have to block so much out if you are going to carry on.'

The court had recently put off the three-day oral hearing on Scot Young's finances until the following April. At that hearing, finally, Young would have to prove what had happened to his money, in detail. If not he was liable go to prison. But that was four months away. Michelle was concerned about how she would make ends meet in the meantime.

'It's a disgrace that women can be treated so badly, where men with money and power can get away with deceit, corruption and the manipulation of other people's lives,' she said.

Scot Young was suffering an exaggerated form of hubris, Michelle believed. He thought he had the Midas touch. Everything he touched turned to gold. He thought he could get away with anything. Now he feared her as his nemesis.

'When Scot Young realised how expensive it would be to divorce me,' she said, 'he went into hiding.'

It was her full-time job now to plough through mountains of legal papers to find out what had happened to the fortune they had built up together.

'Finding where the money has gone has taken over my life,' she said. 'I have no social life. I don't go out, I don't cook, I don't go to the theatre. But I am not going to let him get away with it. What kind of example would that set for my daughters? We need to have faith in the justice system and I pray that the right thing will be done, and done soon.'

Like many women who end up in the divorce courts, she felt that she had given the marriage twenty years of her life. But, more than that, she had been betrayed on so many levels.

'I didn't just raise our daughters,' she said. 'I helped conduct a lot of the business, to build it up, my father advised and helped him. He was just starting out when we met. My family became his family. I may have had a luxury lifestyle and flown in private jets to go on fancy yachts but that's not what's important to me. What's important is looking after my children and making sure they get their education and their future back – the future he has stolen from them.'

By then eighteen-year-old Scarlet had just started work in a clothes shop in the West End, though a career in modelling beckoned. A tall brunette, she was talent-spotted on Miami Beach by an assistant of the American fashion photographer Bruce Webber. However, she said she would rather be finishing her A-levels, or auditioning for Rada, than working.

Scarlet told Ms Brook: 'We don't see ourselves as victims. I may have been stripped of my dignity, but we are just getting on with it.'

She did not want people to feel sorry for her, although some of her friends had not been as supportive as they might have been.

'School girls can be so tricky,' said Michelle.

On the other hand, Michelle complained that her husband was buttressed by male solidarity. He had friends he could turn to for help when he needed to provide his family with living expenses. But even when they had come up with £1 million for school fees and living expenses, they preferred to stay anonymous and her husband refused to say who they were. The courts had to force disclosure. It was only then that she had discovered her mysterious benefactors included Sir Tom Hunter, Sir Philip Green and Richard Caring.

All that money had gone on school fees, living expenses and rent, she said. But the nub of the problem was to discover where the £400 million had gone that he had merely four years ago.

'All we are asking now is for him to disclose to the courts and tell the truth,' she said. 'He thinks, with all the money and power on his side, he will be able to destroy me, that if he exerts enough pressure I will have a nervous breakdown, or the girls will go back to him.'

But she had the bit between her teeth.

'Scot Young has underestimated me,' she said. 'These tycoons think that money and power can buy everyone, they become delusional, but Scot Young's time is running out. He may be a brilliant businessman, but in terms of emotional intelligence he is an imbecile. Relationships and communication have always been difficult for him.'

The real problem was his violent and unpredictable character.

'He used to have extreme mood swings and sometimes he was vicious,' she said. 'We'd never know what mood he'd be in when he got home. I used to think it was drink, and it could be very frightening. He was a volatile personality, one moment charming, charismatic, the next a manipulative bully. In the end it was the girls' distress that made me leave him.'

More tragedy was to strike. While Michelle had been hunting down the missing assets in an attempt to bring her husband to book, her father died. She had been very close to him. So, too, had her husband, at one time.

'When he died, I felt like half of me had gone,' she said. 'He would be horrified at what's happening, but he knew how cruel Scot Young could be.'

Two years had passed and she still had not allowed herself time to mourn and, looking back, she was bitter.

'I married and loved Scot Young for all the right reasons,' she said. 'But he betrayed me. It's not just the money, there are lots of personal belongings missing, too. He pretends he has nothing, yet friends tell me they've seen him in restaurants with different women on his arm.'

She has been told that he was trying to punish her.

'But you cannot punish the mother without punishing the children,' she said. 'What a cruel tactic to punish your children by stopping their education. The law must change. It must protect the children torn apart by these situations.'

Her daughter Sasha said: 'All this has made me doubt his love for me. How could it not?'

The pressure began to tell on Noelle. In May 2011, she moved out of the Bayswater flat she shared with Scot.

'We are no longer an item,' she said.

At a VO5 Extreme Style party in Marylebone, she told the *Daily Mail*: 'Yes, we are no longer living together, but we talk on the phone every day and still see each other as friends. He is the kindest, most generous man I have ever met – you don't have to spend money on a person to be generous.'

She said she wanted to concentrate on her career. Along with being a presenter on Fashion TV, she helped re-launch the Playboy Club in London. She also teamed up with US jeweller Carole Tanenbaum, whose customers included Michelle Obama.

'I'm working sixteen hours a day and simply don't have time for any men,' she said. But this proved to be just another swing of the pendulum in what turned out to be a long-running off-again, on-again affair.

CHAPTER 9

THE X FACTOR

Michelle then got a stroke of luck when the walls of secrecy began crumbling around Scot's super-rich pals. A chink of light appeared. The labyrinthine web of off-shore business interests of property tycoon Kevin Cash, said to be worth up to £500 million, were revealed by his former butler who was taking him to an employment tribunal for unfair dismissal. Cash had paid almost £200,000 to Michelle when the divorce had started and Scot had been best man at Cash's third wedding.

'Kevin Cash was my husband's best friend for many years,' she said. 'They shared many interests as well as business. They operated a system, with others in their set, whereby nothing is held in their names in this country, even though they are British citizens and live here permanently.'

The butler Francesco de Sousa and his wife claimed that they were unfairly dismissed and in a written statement for an employment tribunal de Sousa said he had reported Cash to the taxman over the manner in which he had been paid as an estate manager.

Until they were sacked, the de Sousas worked at North Aston Hall, a £16-million mansion near Bicester, Oxfordshire, which was the country residence of Cash and his wife, South African swimwear model Carla la Reservee, once voted the sexiest woman in South Africa by *FHM* magazine. The de Sousas were claiming £140,000 in compensation after losing their live-in jobs and their accommodation on the estate.

A spokesman for Cash said de Sousa had been dismissed for gross misconduct. Nevertheless, his allegations threw light on the lifestyle and business activities of the publicity-shy Cash and his circle, which included Scot Young and Simon Cowell.

By 2011, Cowell had made *The Sunday Times* Rich List with an estimated fortune of £200 million, making him the sixth richest in the music business, ahead of Elton John and Mick Jagger. He split his time between his home in West London and his mansion in Beverley Hills.

Although Cash admits to having £550 million, his name does not appear on *The Sunday Times* Rich List. He was far too discreet for that. It was only his private life that attracted attention.

Cash has been married four times. His third wife, former page three girl Jackie St Clair, later became Cowell's girlfriend. However, his friends insisted he was not a playboy, saying he was too dedicated to making money to have time to chase women.

One colleague said: 'He handles money for many super-rich businessmen and has managed to make himself more than any of them.'

The same thing was said of Scot Young.

Brought up in Birmingham, Cash began as a trader selling

frozen foods. He survived bankruptcy at the age of eighteen to become a millionaire by his late twenties, when he began buying 'super-prime' London property. In the mid-1990s, he began investing in internet firms, founding Xtream Networks, which was sold in 2002 for more than £70 million. Then he went back into the property business, setting up the Bluestar property group, which bought and sold top London residences. The company brochure claimed it made 'spectacular rates of return' by riding the capital's spiralling property market.

North Aston Hall was owned by Cash's family trust, Rose Property Holdings. The tycoon had no management role in the trust and stayed in North Aston Hall as a 'non-paying resident'. He claimed to own no property in the UK except for a house in Regent's Park, though it has been reported that he owned six properties there. He had the use of a residence in South Africa, but that was owned by his wife's family trust. He was also thought to be behind huge tourist resorts being built near Paris and in Madeira. Despite his extensive business interests and substantial personal wealth, he did not have any British-registered companies.

This was because much of Cash's business empire seems to have been off-shore, saving millions of pounds in tax. The trust that owned at least part of his Oxfordshire estate, for example, was run via a company in Switzerland and registered in the Caribbean tax haven of the British Virgin Islands, where companies do not have to file public accounts or list their directors. Cash was merely a 'consultant' to the trust. But in a statement submitted to the tribunal in Reading, de Sousa said Cash told him he owned about two hundred student properties in Lincolnshire.

When de Sousa appeared in court, he said that Cash had flown out of control when he served his dinner of roast chicken an hour early. According to de Sousa, he had produced the meal at the time Cash's wife had asked for it. Following him back to the kitchen, Cash was said to have kicked open the door and yelled at the couple: 'Get out now! You're fired. Go and find another job.'

Later when de Sousa and his wife met Cash to discuss how much he owed them, he was just as unreasonable.

'He lost his temper again and he said that if we took him to a tribunal we would lose because he has the best lawyers in England and he would make our lives hell,' de Sousa told the tribunal. 'He said he would throw us out on the streets.'

The couple, who lived in a cottage on the estate with their two daughters, were told to leave the following day.

This behaviour was not unusual for Cash, de Sousa said.

'He was very demanding. If anything was not to his liking he would get in a rage,' he said.

The de Sousas, who were from Portugal, revealed more about Cash's lavish lifestyle. He once paid £2,205 for fireworks on Bonfire Night and spent up to £50,000 a month on food and other household necessities. However, the de Sousas said that they were expected to pay for Cash's shopping before being reimbursed, sometimes with cheques from his personal account.

While the de Sousas each worked seventy hours a week in a variety of roles – including butler, estate manager, dog walker, babysitter, cleaner, cook and chauffeur – they were jointly paid just £2,600 a month, net of tax and national insurance, with a further £1,000 net paid each month by cash or cheque on an 'erratic basis'.

At the time they left, the de Sousas claimed that Cash owed them around £14,000 in unpaid bills. Michael Slater, a former solicitor, chairman of Charlton Athletic football club and associate of Mr Cash, had shouted 'You're fired' three times at the couple, alleging they had stolen a laptop and car belonging to Cash, the couple said.

According to de Sousa, when they complained later about their treatment, Cash told them that he could not fire them as he did not own the house. They had to meet a representative of another firm to discuss the end of their employment, but he said that the company had already agreed to sack them.

De Sousa said this was the first time he had been informed that he was not employed by Cash, but by Oakmere Property Management Ltd. After declining a request to attend a meeting with the company's lawyer, the de Sousas were told they were being fired for gross misconduct.

James Wynne, representing the de Sousas, suggested that Cash controlled a variety of companies at 'arm's length', and that the company which nominally employed Mr de Sousa was 'directed in the same way that he directs all the other companies in his business empire'. Cash was a very rich man who funnelled his wealth into off-shore havens to minimise his tax liabilities. He used these companies as a smokescreen. It was clear that he owned them and he was in charge.

'We say it's a sham,' said Mr Wynne. 'Mr Cash did act as if he owned North Aston Hall. He did act as if he was the employer.'

David Flood, representing Cash who was not present at the tribunal, said: 'It appears that the claimant is attempting to use this tribunal as a form of effectively putting him on trial generally as to his business and financial dealings, and using as justification the claimant's own decision not to accept that he was employed by a company rather than Mr Cash. It's going to lead this tribunal into something akin to an overarching conspiracy theory.'

The question the tribunal had to decide was whether the

de Sousas were employed by Cash or by Oakmere Property Management Limited; the name appeared on the de Sousas' bank statements throughout their employment. It had taken over from a company called Beyond North Limited.

A lawyer representing Mr Cash said his client was not registered as a director or shareholder at Companies House and that information about business dealings in the British Virgin Islands was not available to the public.

But de Sousa insisted that Cash was 'a shadow director of the companies in the UK and owner of parent companies incorporated in the British Virgin Islands'.

David Flood, Mr Cash's lawyer, asked de Sousa if he could back up his allegations and challenged him to produce evidence that proved Mr Cash owned either Oakmere Property Management or Beyond North. De Sousa said he could not but insisted: 'I'm certain that Mr Cash did, as he talked about them so many times.'

Flood then asked de Sousa if he had not noticed his wages were being paid by Oakmere Property Management Limited.

'I never paid attention to who paid our wages,' said de Sousa. 'It was only after we were dismissed that we realised we were being paid by all the different companies. Rich people use companies to pay for their expenses.'

Cash did eventually appear at the tribunal to address the cause of the sacking. It appeared that his wife, Carla, had asked for dinner to be serve at 6 pm, while Cash had expected to be eating at 7 pm.

'It was a misunderstanding,' Cash explained, but de Sousa would not leave it at that.

'He wouldn't leave it alone,' Cash said, 'and was being very derogatory of Carla. I didn't shout but I did raise my voice. It was a heated argument. I told him to get out of the house, or words to that effect. I didn't want to spend my Saturday night having a circular conversation about a chicken.'

Cash had fresh allegations over the sacking of de Sousa.

'He had a problem of jealousy of my relationship with Carla,' he told the tribunal. 'He had an over-inflated version of his relationship with me. I think he has a problem with me.'

The mix-up over the dinner was a 'trivial matter', Cash maintained, but de Sousa had 'overstepped the mark'. He then went into detail about what had happened.

'At 6 pm Francisco told us that dinner was ready.' Cash said. 'When I indicated that I thought we were eating at 7 pm, he told me that Carla had indicated that she wanted to eat at 6 pm.'

Cash insisted that Carla had asked for dinner to be served at 7 pm.

'I informed him that this was not what Carla had said but that I didn't really care,' said Cash. 'Francisco then became strangely upset. Francisco said that I would not believe him over Carla because I was sleeping with Carla. I did not shout but I did raise my voice and I recall saying something along the lines of, "I've had enough of this. I don't want you in the house. Get out."'

Cash continued to deny that he was the couple's employer and was consequently therefore not liable for their sacking. He also said that documents produced at the tribunal had been stored in the bottom of a locked wardrobe which de Sousa had keys to.

'He stole those documents and they were only returned to me after a threat of injunction by my solicitors,' Cash said.

No more about Cash's foreign dealings that Michelle Young so desperately wanted to hear about came out. The papers de Sousa had found were no longer in his possession and the de Sousas lost the case.

The employment tribunal said that Mr Cash was not 'someone who would care very much about the time he ate a meal', but had reacted to Mr de Sousa's criticism of his wife Carla, and told him to get out of the house.

'We find that Mr Cash did not want Mr de Sousa to be part of his household after he had spoken rudely and disrespectfully about Mrs Cash,' said Peter Lewis, the tribunal judge.

The tribunal found that the de Sousas had not been unfairly dismissed and that Cash had never been responsible for their employment.

'I'm pleased justice has been done,' said Cash. The case had been 'unwarranted, untrue and, as expected, unsuccessful'.

The Cash case had not come up with any pay dirt, though it had added to Mrs Young's suspicions that her husband's money was hidden off-shore. Like Young, Kevin Cash was, on paper at least, penniless in the UK, while he was plainly very rich indeed. But next time she appeared in High Court, she levelled her sights on Simon Cowell, claiming that he was one of three millionaires who aided Scot Young in keeping more than £2 billion in assets secret from the court hearings. The other two, Topshop owner Sir Philip Green and restaurant entrepreneur Richard Caring, had come up in the case before. Now Cowell was being dragged in. He was furious and said he would consider suing over the 'utterly untrue' claims.

Representing himself, Mr Young again asked: 'Who is hiding my assets?'

She replied: 'Sir Philip Green, Simon Cowell and Richard Caring.'

Michelle claimed that Boris Berezovsky was also involved in the conspiracy. By then, Berezovsky had been granted political asylum in Britain. The former British ambassador Sir Andrew Wood described Berezovsky as 'an extremely useful channel into the Kremlin and beyond it' who had been 'a demonstrative friend of British interests'. That help had included obtaining the release of two British hostages held by Chechen gangs in 1998. He then used Britain as a safe haven in his attempt to bring down Putin through the International Foundation for Civil Liberties, which he had established, further annoying Putin by funding his enemies in the Ukraine – including backing the 'Orange Revolution' in November 2005.

Attempts to have him extradited back to Russia failed. In 2007, a Moscow court found that Berezovsky was a member of an 'organised criminal group' that stole Aeroflot's foreign currency and convicted him of embezzling 215 million roubles (£4.3 million) from the company, sentencing him to six years in jail, *in absentia*. Another court sentenced him to another thirteen years for defrauding Autovaz of 58 million roubles (£1.3 million). Berezovsky dismissed the convictions as 'a farce'. They were widely seen as politically motivated. Nevertheless, Berezovsky was investigated in several other jurisdictions for money laundering.

His life was also in danger. When attending Bow Street magistrates' court to face extradition hearings on the embezzlement charges, an assassin was said to have planned to kill him with a poison-filled fountain pen when he arrived at court.

'From the beginning when I moved to this country I got several threatening letters, signed Ivan Ivanovich, Nikolai Nikolavic,' Berezovsky said. 'It's just the signature of the KGB, they did not hide it.'

In June 2007, Scotland Yard advised Berezovsky to leave the country as an assassin was on his way from Russia to kill him. The murder attempt was planned to take place in the London Hilton. However, the hit man was picked up and deported.

Berezovsky said he was told 'that someone who I know will come to London to meet me, he will kill me openly, without any hiding, and he will explain later that it's just business reasons. He will spend ten years in jail, will be released, will have a lot of money, and will be a hero of Russia.'

Berezovsky returned when the police gave him the all-clear. Others had also been in danger. The North London home of Berezovsky's associate, the former prime minister of the secessionist Chechen Republic of Ichkeria, Akhmed Zakayev, was guarded by a squad of uniformed officers and Litvinenko's widow Marina was told to take precautions.

While Berezovsky had managed to stay out of the courts in Russia, he became quite a familiar figure in the High Court in London. He sued the American business magazine *Forbes* when it said that he was a Russian mafia boss. The case was settled when *Forbes* offered a partial retraction, saying that Berezonsky had not been responsible for murder.

He also sued fellow oligarch Mikhail Fridman, head of the industrial and financial Alfa Group, for slander when Fridman said Berezovsky had threatened to kill him when the two were vying for control of the Kommersant publishing house. The jury was split 10-1 in favour of Berezovsky because they said Fridman had failed to present convincing evidence that Berezovsky had threatened to kill him.

In 2006, the *Guardian* apologised to Berezovsky after accusing him of fraud. He was awarded another £150,000 against Russian state channel RTR Planeta who had accused him of being behind the murder of Mr Litvinenko. The broadcaster did not even participate in the hearings, allowing a sole source to defend himself in court.

Then in 2011, Berezovsky sued Abramovich for £3 billion, accusing his former partner of blackmailing him into selling his interest in Sibneft, the oil company and aluminium con-glomerate they started together, at a knock-down price. This became the biggest civil court case in British legal history, dwarfing even the Youngs' divorce case.

After all, Mrs Young only claimed her husband was worth £400 million when they split and she was still hoping for a £200 million divorce payout. Meanwhile, he continued to insist that he was broke, even though he had recently been spotted driving a Ferrari. It was a car he could easily afford, she maintained, because he had the backing of Green, Cowell, Caring and Berezovsky.

Addressing Mrs Young, Family Division judge Mr Justice Mostyn said: 'You say these people are helping him hide his money?'

'Yes,' she replied.

He then asked if she was saying there was 'a huge conspiracy involving a lot of people, who would otherwise be regarded as respectable, to hide his assets'?

Again she said: 'Yes.'

Then Judge Mostyn warned her: 'You have to be careful when you make serious allegations that well-known people have been involved in criminal conspiracy. Do you under-stand that?'

'Absolutely, my lord,' Mrs Young said.

The allegations got more serious when she was asked whether she was suggesting those named were intending 'to pervert and defeat the course of justice'. She replied: 'Yes.'

Mrs Young then claimed that her husband was 'a secret major shareholder' in Simon Cowell's TV show *American Idol*.

Judge Mostyn asked: 'Are they hiding other assets of signifi-cant value other than *American Idol*?'

'Yes,' said Mrs Young, 'but I am told I will never find out the truth because these people are wealthy and powerful.'

Looking directly at her husband, she added: 'I am sure you are not going to tell the truth are you?'

Outside the court, a spokesman for Simon Cowell said: 'These allegations are completely untrue and our lawyers are contacting Mrs Young about her statements.'

Berezovsky also said: 'The claims are completely false and ludicrous.'

Mrs Young also claimed that the £200,000 given to her by Sir Philip Green was, in fact, her husband's money. Her lawyer Philip Noble said a list of Mr Young's assets had been found on a hard disk he tried to wipe clean. It was clear who had the money. He was now living with his girlfriend, model and actress Noelle Reno, in Knightsbridge, while his wife was living in a two-bedroom flat in Victoria with her daughters.

Mr Noble told the court: 'Mr Young says he is penniless. He says he has debts to his friends of £28 million. He has, according to him, no physical means of support... He says he has £150 income a week, although he goes out to very expensive restaurants like Cipriani and The Ivy.'

Mrs Young maintained that her husband used a variety of different pseudonyms, had concealed his assets in off-shore accounts in Switzerland, Paris, the Bahamas and the British Virgin Islands. She told the High Court that her husband had claimed poverty when in fact he continued to work and had set up property deals in Mayfair and Moscow that earned millions.

'He was,' she said, 'a genius, super-intelligent – and as the years went on sometimes overbearing.'

She may have been overestimating his abilities, but he was certainly proving a formidable adversary. When Mr Young went into the witness box, the judge told him that his wife had made 'some quite serious allegations about these famous people holding enormous amounts of assets'.

Young, who admitted to being on anti-depressants, accused his wife of being a fantasist. He insisted he had only seen Sir Philip Green twice in the past two years, once outside a nightclub and had had business dealings with him only on the one other occasion.

'Simon Cowell I have seen on less than five occasions in my life,' he said. 'I have never had any business with him. I believe this is just the work of a fantasist. It's mind-boggling. I categorically say that I don't have any secret share-holding in *American Idol* – it's laughable, my lord.'

However, Young admitted he was living in a £4,300-a-month flat in central London, but said it was being paid for by a friend. Young said that his wife's claim that the £200,000 given to her by Sir Philip Green was actually 'ludicrous'. He had not had an income since 2006 and had just £265 and a tube ticket in his pockets. He said he could not work because he was suffering from depression.

It was noticeable that he was no longer wearing the slick suits he had been seen in when he had first been pictured in the company of Ms Reno. In court, he was wearing a cheap black T-shirt and a black baseball cap, and was unshaven.

The court also heard that Sir Tom Hunter paid her £104,000-a-year rent as part of handouts totalling £1.1 million. Asked why friends had given large sums to his wife after they split, Young said: 'Because she was destitute, she had nowhere to live.'

The cash was paid over an eighteen-month period starting in 2007 by his friends who thought she would spend it 'wisely', he said. 'They certainly did not think she was going to spend it on lawyers.'

He said the payments ended in around 2008 after his relationship with his wife had 'irretrievably broken down'.

His friends had certainly not intended to provide her with a meal-ticket for life and, by then, they had expected him to bounce back.

'There was a level to where people would go and they had reached that level,' he said. 'They thought I would have pulled my boot straps up by then and they were not going to indefinitely support my wife.'

However, his wealthy friends continued to support him. One friend, Justin Williams, had paid around £71,000 towards his £4,300-a-month flat in Lancaster Gate in London, the court heard.

'He is a wealthy chap, a very good friend who thinks I have been vilified and tried to help,' Young said.

When shown a Coutts bank statement from 2002, he was asked about £17.5 million in cash which was then available.

'I can't remember having that in my bank account,' he said.

Despite all Mrs Young's hard work, mystery still surrounded the whereabouts of his assets. The HMRC was doing no better. The week before the hearing Young was due to be discharged from his backruptcy, but the trustee had refused to discharge him due to his 'lack of co-operation'.

Simon Cowell was so outraged by Mrs Young's 'scandalous' allegations that the following day he sent a barrister and libel lawyers from the expensive law firm Carter Ruck to the hearings at the High Court.

Representing Cowell, Matthew Nicklin said his client was horrified by the claims made against him, which he heard for the first time that week.

'As a result of the privilege attaching to reports of court proceedings and the immunity Mrs Young enjoys for what she says as a witness in the witness box, Mr Cowell has absolutely no redress against the re-publication of her allegations,' said

Nicklin. 'They are scandalous. I am here today to make clear that Mr Cowell categorically refutes the claims made against him by Mrs Young. Mr Cowell has had no opportunity to defend himself against these allegations. They are in his submission scandalous. He has never had any business dealings with Mr Young and has no knowledge whatsoever of Mr Young's financial affairs. The allegation that Mr Young is a secret shareholder in *American Idol* is simply false. Mr Cowell would never be a party to any attempt to mislead the court and the allegations made by Ms Young are completely without foundation.'

Mr Justice Mostyn agreed, saying he did not believe that there was any financial link between Scot Young and Simon Cowell.

'If I was to give a preliminary judgement, I would say there is not a scrap of evidence that Simon Cowell is sheltering funds or shares in the way that is urged,' the judge said.

He then asked Philip Noble, Mrs Young's barrister, if she was considering abandoning her claim. From the back of the court, Mrs Young said loudly: 'No, I am not... Investigations are continuing.'

Mr Noble admitted that his client had named Cowell because he moved in the same social circles as her husband and the other well-known figures she had identified in court. She did not have any further evidence against Mr Cowell 'apart from what she views in her own mind as guilt by association,' he said.

The judge ruled that, if Mrs Young wanted him to make a formal finding about her husband's involvement with 'the music impresario' Mr Cowell, he would have to be given at least two weeks' notice. Her barrister said that he had been instructed that Mr Cowell would not be called to give evidence.

CONSPIRACY OF SILENCE

Cowell's barrister said that he was grateful to the judge for making it clear that there 'was no evidence to support the allegations' Mrs Young had made previously. He was off the hook – if, indeed, he had ever been on it.

CHAPTER 10

DEALS WITHIN DEALS

Among the records retrieved from the hard drive of the computer Young had given to his daughters was a document which purported to show he still owned a substantial amount of property in London, as well as a hall of residence at the University of Lincoln. Young denied this. Mr Justice Mostyn had highlighted a reference on the files to a property at 56 Curzon Street, Mayfair, which he then read out: 'Sale about to be exchanged. Scot Young will own a hundred per cent of this property.'

Turning to Mr Young, he asked: 'What does that mean?'

Young replied: 'I was looking at buying it. I was going to try and borrow some money. But the deal fell through due to lack of finance.'

The judge was sceptical.

'You wouldn't have written that unless you had the finance in place,' he said. 'Was it some fantasy? Had you lined up any finance?'

'I genuinely tried to do the deal,' Young replied.

The next day, Kevin Cash was dragged into the case when the High Court heard from Mr Young's former solicitor, Stanley Beller. He had fallen out with the property dealer after Young had allegedly reneged on a business deal that had left the lawyer owing hundreds of thousands of pounds.

Beller claimed that Cash had only become wealthy after meeting Young. They were such good friends that Young had been best man at Cash's marriage to the South African model Carla La Reservee. But while Cash managed to hold on to his fortune, Young lost his.

'Kevin Cash and Scot Young became business partners in the late 1990s,' Beller told the court. 'When I first met him, Kevin Cash had zero assets. Following his relationship with Scot Young, he appears to be a very wealthy man.'

It was alleged that Cash had helped 'shield' his friend's wealth.

Philip Noble, representing Mrs Young, asked Mr Beller if there was any inference to be deduced from the contrasting fortunes of the two men.

'I know they were in partnership together,' he said. 'I can only tell you what I knew until March 2006. They were involved in a number of transactions together involving telecoms and property.'

The court was also told that Mr Cash was another of Scot Young's friends who had provided financial maintenance to Mrs Young after their separation.

Still trying to ascertain Scot Young's actual worth, Mr Justice Mostyn asked: 'You say that the £7.6 million [sic] debt is fake, that's what you are saying?'

'Yes, my lord,' Beller replied

He told the court that his professional life had been left

in tatters after Mr Young removed share certificates from his office without his consent. This left him 'in the lurch' and he was struck off as a solicitor in 2007.

Young, representing himself, accused Beller of lying and said he was giving evidence to settle a 'personal vendetta'. But the matter was left hanging when Mr Justice Mostyn adjourned the case until October, giving the adversaries six months to cool off, in the hope that they would come to some kind of agreement. Despite four days' testimony in the High Court, no progress had been made to find out how much Scot Young was worth, or where his money had gone.

Outside the court Beller had managed to drag BBC Director General Mark Thompson into the case. Beller told the *Mail on Sunday* that he had been present when Young had arranged a meeting between Thompson and his business partner Poju Zabludowicz, who was also chairman of the Britain Israel Communications and Research Centre, an organisation which lobbies the government on behalf of Israel, at Drones, a private members club in Mayfair in July 2005.

The arrangements were confused and Beller said that Young had offered him the table he had booked for himself.

'Scot said he couldn't make the reservation but I should take my wife Michelle as he would pick up the tab,' he said. 'We were in the restaurant when, to our surprise, Scot walked in at about 9.30 pm with two men. He waved to us and they went to sit in the far corner.'

The whole thing was very mysterious.

'We couldn't understand why he was there when he had given us his reservation,' Beller continued. 'They placed their orders and seemed to be having an animated discussion. After a while, Scot came over and invited us to join them for a coffee. He introduced us to Mr Zabludowicz and a businessman, who said he was chairman of a leading Israeli football club. I can't recall his name. The conversation started on football, then politics, and one of the men complained that Israel was always getting bad publicity in Britain. They insisted the BBC was anti-Israel. Scot bragged that the guy running the BBC was his "good mate" and they were neighbours who often dined together.'

According to Beller, Young picked up his mobile and asked if Thompson would pop over to meet some people. He had no idea who Thompson was at the time.

'Fifteen minutes later, he was sitting down having a drink with us. I was most impressed to see that Scot could just ring the DG of the BBC and get him to drop everything just like that,' said Beller. 'Mr Thompson explained that he had been working late. He ended up defending the BBC's position and volunteered that his wife was Jewish. When he revealed that he had never visited Israel, the two businessmen fell over themselves to invite him as their guest. Both said they could introduce him to people who mattered.'

At the time, the BBC was facing strong criticism for apparently favouring Palestinians in its news coverage of the Middle East conflict. Mr Thompson refused to release the result of an internal report into the claims, which was completed in November that year. By then, Thompson travelled with his wife to Israel for three days, where he held talks with the then Prime Minister Ariel Sharon, which were supposedly intended to let the BBC 'build bridges with Israel'. He also met Palestinian president Mahmoud Abbas.

When the *Mail on Sunday* ran with the story, Young confirmed that the meeting at Drones had taken place, but he said he could not recall the precise content of the conversation.

'I called Mark because he was in the area and he joined us

for a drink. It was a long time ago and I don't remember all the detail,' he said.

Since the divorce case hit the headlines, Young had lost touch with Thompson.

'Mark was a family friend,' said Young. 'He is a great cook and would often invite us over for meals. But I've only seen him once in the past four years. There has been no bust-up.'

The BBC was more circumspect.

'We are not going to discuss private meetings which may or may not have taken place,' said a spokesman. 'The trip to Israel is already in the public domain. But any suggestion or allegation of undue influence being asserted will be taken very seriously by us.'

Beller and Young fell out when the tycoon's business empire started to collapse in 2006. Beller was struck off by the Law Society in 2007 after being found guilty of failing to comply with professional undertakings given on behalf of Young. In 2009, Lord Justice Thomas refused to renew Beller's licence and described Young as 'a man who is dishonest', who had duped his lawyer.

While Mrs Young was not intending to pursue Simon Cowell any further in court, she remained adamant that he and Sir Philip Green had conspired to help Scot. She told *The Times*: 'They all went to party on their private yachts and eat in Cipriani. Money, power and secrecy binds them all together.'

Again, it was guilt by association.

She admitted that they were generous to her after the couple split because Scot was 'a player – in telecoms, the film industry, property, shares. He was friends with everyone. If you investigate the Richard Caring property deals in Mayfair, you'll find Scot Young behind most of them'.

But a friend of Caring said that Scot had never been involved in any of his property deals and that Caring had only ever invested in one company with Scot. It was an IT venture that had failed.

Sir Philip Green also distanced himself. A source close to Sir Philip said that the retailer had paid Michelle's estate agent about £80,000 – not £200,000 – for rent. Nor was he close to Scot.

'He knows the guy through a wider circle of friends but they have never had any business together,' the source said.

Even Sir Tom Hunter, who admitted to being a friend of Scot's, denied having any business dealings with him.

And Stanley Beller's insinuation that Kevin Cash had become suddenly suspiciously wealthy when Young's fortune had gone missing? Allies said most of Cash's estimated £500-million wealth came from family trusts.

'The accusations in court against Kevin are laughable, ludicrous and lamentable,' a friend said. 'Kevin and Scot were best friends. But now he's keeping his distance. Everyone is being tainted by these allegations.'

Young complained that he was being shunned by his former business associates thanks to the divorce case. He said that his wife's courtroom antics were making it virtually impossible for him to rebuild his business career because many associates, new and old, were now wary of dealing with him.

'Her scurrilous accusations are doing me no favours in the business community,' he maintained.

The courtroom disclosures had infuriated fellow business-men, who detest the public discussion of their private finances. Friends refused to offer any more to help and cut back most – if not all – contact with Young himself.

Green said he had hardly spoken to Young in the past two years, while Cash and Young, formerly close business allies, had met just five times in five years – and only then by chance, as they used the same swish restaurants.

Jaeger boss Harold Tillman, who according to court papers gave £92,000 to Michelle Young to help with rent and other costs, began telling friends he could hardly recall having met Young.

'This sort of publicity is causing Scot a great deal of damage with his business contacts,' a close friend told *The Sunday Times*. 'Some of them have stopped talking to him altogether.'

But Michelle was unconvinced.

'I don't believe he has lost business associates and friends as a result of this case,' she said.

Michelle Young's former lawyer, Ayesha Vardag, said: 'Divorce cases rake up all sorts of dirty linen, and now the parties can expect this to be aired in the press.'

However, there were new people in town and even the dressed-down Scot made an impression in some quarters. One acquaintance said: 'He's a bit scruffy – sometimes unshaven, wearing a baseball cap and jeans. He's typical of a breed of networkers in their late thirties and forties who come to London and make a lot of money by manipulating the system. They all have stunning model girlfriends and a collection of luxury cars with designer number plates. They are a version of the Russian oligarchs. On the other hand, Young is quite a complicated character. He's an amenable bloke who is very good at listening and getting you to talk. He has a sympathetic touch and you feel quite sorry for him in a way. I've seen him become hysterical on one occasion.'

Nevertheless he was seen at the lunch to celebrate the Carole Tanenbaum jewellery collection, co-hosted by Noelle Reno at the five-star Baglioni Hotel in Kensington. Here he was among peers. He shared a table with film producer Lisa Tchenguiz who was demanding £100 million in a divorce settlement from multi-millionaire fruit-juice tycoon Vivian Imerman. Like Scot, her brothers were in property development. It is not known whether they were talking about property or divorce.

'They were just exchanging war stories,' said another guest.

Meanwhile, more luck came Michelle's way when, in January 2012, an anonymous donor – one of several to offer help – gave her money to continue her fight. Friends said that, initially, she would have £3 million to play with, but more could be made available if necessary. She hired a new legal team that included Sofia Dionissiou-Moussaoui of DWFM Beckman Solicitors and Deborah Bangay, QC, who is described on her website as a 'big money' divorce lawyer and famed for achieving a record-breaking settlement for footballer Ray Parlour's wife. They would be key to winning her case, Michelle believed.

'I've had a lot of interest from funders,' said Michelle. 'Four or five wanted to fund the case. We chose the one we felt was most secure. It's an open fund, meaning we can basically have as much money as we want. I'm relieved and positive. I think it's going to be an interesting year.'

This time it was Mrs Young who went to the High Court to ask for an adjournment of the forthcoming hearings.

'I have the right team and correct amount of funding,' said Michelle. 'We need an adjournment for the team to prepare.'

She said the name of the backer would be revealed at the end of the case, but confirmed it was not one of Mr Young's friends who had helped her in the past. There was speculation that her backer was not an individual but a hedge fund that would demand thirty per cent of her award, if she won the case. Young declined to identify the mystery donor, but said that previous backers had asked for as much as forty per cent.

Now she said she was not being asked for a percentage but for a fixed fee, which she refused to disclose. Harbour Litigation Funding had backed out after failing to agree the terms of its cut. Mrs Young thought it was wrong that she had to make these deals to continue to pursue her errant husband.

'It's an injustice that I have to go through this process just to get justice,' she said. 'Unless you are rich you just can't win this type of case. I'm very grateful my case is being funded. Without it, I would have been screwed.'

Once again, she was confident of success.

'For me and my children, it will be justice after all this suffering,' she said. 'We have been to Hell and back. There are many women in this country whose wealthy husbands are hiding assets off-shore. For Scot Young, this has been a complete power trip.'

Claiming that it was he who was now without funding, Young said he was happy to represent himself in court. A friend told *The Times* that his wife's new benefactor would make no difference.

'It doesn't change anything because there is no money to find,' they said. 'Scot doesn't care who the backer is. He hasn't got any money for them to take anyway. If she finds it, she can have it all because there's nothing.'

By then, the couple's younger daughter Sasha had been forced to leave her £14,400–a-year girls' day school, Francis Holland. She was reportedly looking for a publisher for what she described as a 'self-help children's novel'.

'I wouldn't want anyone to go through what my sister and I have been through,' seventeen-year-old Sasha told *Mail Online*. She had eight GCSEs and wanted to go on to take her A-levels, perhaps back at Francis Holland if her mother ever won the money she thought she was due.

'I am still hoping something good will happen out of the next hearing and that I can go back to studying,' she said. 'I know my situation is not the norm, but I still think I have something to say to help others. I have learned a lot. I think I can help others. I am aiming the book at eight- to thirteen-year-olds.'

She had a very clear idea of the task ahead of her.

'I don't want to write a boring book of bullet points on how to deal with your parents' marriage break-up and divorce,' she said. 'I don't think anyone would read that. So I am writing it in the form of a children's novel with two main characters, who will be the children in a story based on all my real-life experiences.'

Her mother gave her her full backing.

'I am proud of my daughters,' Michelle said. 'Scarlet has had to leave school, too, and she is working as a model. Sasha's book is brilliant.'

Perhaps gaining inspiration from his daughter, Scot was trying to move on too. He went back to the family court and asked Mr Justice Mostyn to give him his passport back as he wanted to take up a business opportunity in Africa that involved a charity.

'I want to re-start my career,' said Young, 'I want to get back to work and to provide for my family. I have two daughters I love. I am working to get my life back in shape. I need the opportunity to travel. I want to resurrect my career and get back to work. And that would be to the benefit of all, including my family.'

He said that he had substantially complied with his legal obligations and attended every court hearing, even when he had been out of the jurisdiction. The retention of his passport was a clear breach of his human rights.

Michelle Young's counsel, Edward Fitzgerald QC, opposed this, saying his passport should stay confiscated while a forensic accountant examined his finances. Mr Fitzgerald said that no human rights issues were involved. The charity mentioned by Mr Young had existed since 2003 and had nothing to do with him.

'Despite the pathetic figure Mr Young seeks to present in court, we suggest he is thoroughly dishonest,' he said. 'He had £400 million in 2006 and hasn't explained where it has gone. The wife will be denied any chance of justice at all if he goes abroad. The fact is, this is someone who is an accomplished deceiver, and when he says he is just going abroad for this business opportunity, we invite the court to be deeply sceptical.'

After considering the matter for a week, Mr Justice Mostyn decided to retain Young's passport as 'plainly' he wanted to flee the court's jurisdiction.

'His asserted intention to travel to Africa to engage in charity work strikes me as highly implausible,' said the judge, 'and I consider that there must be some ulterior reason for his wish to leave the country. I am wholly satisfied that were Mr Young to depart, Mrs Young would be materially prejudiced in the prosecution of her claim for financial remedies.'

The judge went on to say that Young was 'grossly in contempt' of court in relation to his maintenance payments and that it was 'hardly an excuse for him to rely on his bankruptcy. He had heard evidence in an earlier hearing to the effect that Mr Young continued to live at his Bayswater flat, where the monthly rent of £4,000, along with the council tax and utility bills was paid for by a friend. He carried around as much at £400 in his pocket and friends had given him thousands in cash.

Young was also still in contempt of court for not having fulfilled his obligations on disclosure.

'It is for him to show that he has fully complied with his disclosure obligations, not for Mrs Young to show that he has not,' the judge said. A mantra that "I believe I have complied" does not amount to a clear demonstration of compliance.'

This gave Michelle a boost. She was now so confident of victory that she was telling the papers she wanted to go into business helping divorcing women, by working with an investment company who would fund legal cases in exchange for a stake in the final settlement.

'I want to be a pioneer for others in my position,' she said. 'When I started on this journey, I had no idea which lawyers, which QC and which forensic accountants to use. Now I know this area from the inside, possibly better than anyone. Women have to go through so much to get the assets that are rightfully theirs. There is a need for a service that gives advice and can offer a fair way to fund legal proceedings. I would use my contacts to get together the best legal professionals.'

She was in a perfect position to do this, she told *The Times*, as she had spent huge sums instructing lawyers and accountants. She said that some divorce lenders were taking advantage of customers.

'Because they know that you are in a vulnerable position and have got no option, they charge enormous fees,' she said.

Her first lender agreed to fund her legal costs in exchange for ten per cent of her winnings. But as the case dragged on, that rose to twenty per cent. Some such lenders take forty or even fifty per cent of winnings, she claimed.

She would still not reveal the details of her last deal with an unnamed backer, other than saying it was a 'commercial agreement'. However, if she won, as she expected, £500 million, her secret backer could walk away with £150 million – a small price to pay. Now she could look to her future victory with confidence and was more relaxed than at any time since the divorce began six years earlier.

'If I had had someone five years ago to offer appropriate funding for me and my daughters, this case would have been over in a year or eighteen months,' she said. 'At the beginning it's so traumatising and time-consuming. It's a full-time job that has stolen six years of our lives. I have been distraught, though the more I read the more confident I became. Other women should not go through that.'

The family justice system, she said, was skewed in favour of men, who are more likely to control the family's finances and better able to use their business acumen to conceal assets. Now with the money on tap, she was once again threatening to call Simon Cowell and Sir Philip Green to give evidence in the case.

CHAPTER 11

DISTANT BELLS

As the case dragged inexorably on with no end in sight, Noelle Reno began to feel sorry for herself.

'It would be really nice if I could be with a guy who could take me shopping, which he can't do,' she rued. 'He's completely broke and all he wants to do is to go and earn money and support his kids.'

But still Young would not – or could not – pay up. He was not downhearted though. In May 2012, he told the *Mail on Sunday*: 'Once it's over I'll marry her the next day if I can. Waiting has been incredibly frustrating. I'm crazy in love and can't wait to get all this nonsense out of the way and have a new life with the woman I want to spend my life with.'

Off to the Cannes film festival, Noelle said: 'There will be one very big, elegant wedding in London. I'd love to do it as soon as possible after November, but the scale that we want it to be will involve a lot of planning. It will be a huge party. I can't wait to have little kiddies.'

Young promised her that they would be wed by Christmas. It seemed a distant prospect. In November 2012, Mr Justice Moor gave Young another twenty-eight days to make a full financial disclosure or face the six-month prison term that was originally handed down in 2009, but had then been suspended. Young had previously been granted a stay of execution until a trial, but the case had then been delayed when his wife had trouble finding the money to pay lawyers and forensic analysts to examine what accounts he had provided.

The judge agreed to overturn the previous ruling suspending the sentence, after Mrs Young argued in court that the case had effectively come to a standstill due to a shortage of money, the illness of a judge and Young's own apparent health problems. But now, those problems were behind them and a full trial was scheduled for the following October.

'The threat of imprisonment is the only thing that will bring him to heel,' said Michelle. 'He has, until now, lied, prevaricated and basically ignored every court order for him to provide a full account of what happened to his money and properties. His aim all along has been to drag it out until I ran out of money.'

Now she had been through tough times and success could not be far away.

'A lot of people took my money, but I never saw any real results,' she said. 'I sold all my jewellery and used all the spare cash that I had to keep things going. Eventually I got some funding, but it was like wading through treacle.'

Her anonymous new backer was convinced by her case. After all, he was willing to gamble £3 million against a hefty slice of her settlement – if there was one.

'I had to lay out my evidence to him, like any business person trying to get a bank loan,' she explained. 'He believed

I had a strong case, or he would not have given me the money.'

After another meeting with her advisers in what she called her 'war room', she said: 'Things are beginning to unravel. We are slowly untangling the paper trail to show that far from being the pauper he pretends, Scot has been "living it large".'

She had identified ten previously unacknowledged properties from her husband's portfolio, held by the prestigious business law firm Fox Williams.

'I didn't even know about these,' she said. 'It's part of the vast list of assets he is supposed to have lost, which are now being released because he wants to avoid going to jail.'

She claimed that her husband had deliberately made himself bankrupt – by the simple expedient of not paying his taxes. But she could show that he still had money even after he had ended up on Carey Street. She had unearthed documents detailing a new banking trust set up for him in the Isle of Man in 2009 and papers showing that he was still involved in multi-million-pound deals.

'There are also two accounts in the names of his friends, through which money is being funnelled for his daily use,' she said. 'That's how he's been funding his lifestyle. I've been told that he pays for everything with wads of cash stuffed in his pocket.'

Much of this new evidence was found during an early-morning raid on a hotel room off the Bayswater Road near Hyde Park in West London the previous March. Michelle's lawyers had secured a search-and-seizure order and high court officials confiscated several cheques. Two amounted to £32,500, although no payee name had been written in. As well as a large amount of paperwork, three laptops and eight mobile phones were seized. To Michelle, the significance of the set-up was plain.

'It was obvious that he was using the place as a makeshift office,' she said. 'The cheques were issued by Baron & Co, a company controlled by George Constantine, a director of several companies owned by Scot and one of his close friends. Mr Constantine has told my lawyers that he was giving money to Scot.'

That same morning court officials carried out simultaneous raids on Noelle Reno's flat and on the offices of Gire House Capital, another law firm used by Young.

With these discoveries, Michelle's new team thought they could put together a clearer picture of where her husband had hidden his wealth.

'I'm truly staggered by the calculated way that he set about making it disappear,' she said. 'He restructured his assets, with layers of elaborate and overlapping trusts in more than twenty countries. It was coldly orchestrated and ruthlessly executed. We have no contact now, but when I see him in court, trying to get the judge's sympathy, I find it hard to believe this is the man I once loved.'

While his primary creditor was HM Revenue & Customs, Young had remained on remarkably friendly terms with several associates to whom he owed substantial sums. And while it was true that some properties had been repossessed, others seemed to have been sold cheaply to friends.

'He has managed to shrink an empire built around some of the most expensive areas of the country,' Michelle said. 'It took a lot of planning, but he could only have done it with the aid of people willing to hold some of those assets.'

Plainly, his associates were helping him hide his fortune.

'One man told us how he kept money in an account for Scot,' Michelle said. 'The cash was then withdrawn over a number of days from various machines. It's called smurfing and is used mainly by criminals.'

It was these types of allegations that prevented him working, Young complained.

'I want to look after my family,' he said. 'But it's been difficult to get back on my feet. I'll do everything possible to comply with the court order. I just want this to be over so that I can get on with rebuilding my career.'

Michelle was unsympathetic.

'This is not just about money,' she said. 'It's also about principles. Some people might say that I've become obsessed, but all I want is justice for myself and our two daughters.'

Yet the slow grind of the legal system was often frustrating. After all, justice delayed is justice denied.

'I'm appalled that he's been able to manipulate it to his own ends,' she said. 'He's failed to produce documents when ordered by the court, claiming to be either suffering from gastric illness or a breakdown. Occasionally I've felt like giving up. But I want to set an example for my girls; to show them that it is important to fight for something when you believe you are in the right. Too many rich men think they can walk away from a long marriage without facing up to their responsibilities.'

Nevertheless, she insisted that a settlement had been possible at any point.

'I would gladly sit down privately and come to an agreement,' she said. 'But he's stubborn.'

It was a case of an irresistible force meeting an immoveable object and Michelle still feared that she might weaken.

'I'm not the woman I once was,' she said. 'I spend my days reading documents – there's a room full of files for this case. I've had to learn a lot about the law, insolvency, bankruptcy, accounting. It's not been easy but, ultimately, I knew my cause was just. Scot and I started out with nothing and built what we had together. I helped to find some of the properties, co-signed documents for loans and managed much of the refurbishment. I did not deserve to be treated like this.'

There were rumours Michelle had started dating, but the well-spring of her strength was a close circle of supportive women friends. What's more, she relished the fight. The days of ease were long behind her but even that brought some benefit.

'My life is more fulfilling,' she said. 'I've learned a lot about myself and have been surprised by my strength and resilience. I want to try to raise awareness and help other women going through the same drama. People said I'd never be able to prove my case, but it's all coming together. There should be a lot of very nervous people at this stage.'

Scot Young was also in good shape and claimed to be ready for any ordeal.

'I gave up alcohol two months ago,' he said. 'I've lost more than a stone. I've not had a drink in ages and I'm getting up early every morning to do my exercise regime.'

He now had a flat stomach and had switched his brand to Marlboro Menthol. For the next hearing he had gone back to wearing a dapper dark suit. It was noted that he seemed to be glowing with health and vitality 'like someone who had just returned from a winter sunshine holiday' – though, of course, without a passport, he hadn't.

A reporter caught him eating a sandwich and sipping a fizzy water in The George pub across the road from the court before the November hearing. He was busting for the next round.

'If I do go to jail, then she's going with me,' he said. 'She's the mother of my children and I don't really want her to go to jail, but if I do, then so will she. What she's doing is illegal. She's been silly and it could land her in jail.'

However, when he claimed in court his wife was hounding

him, the judge told him these allegations had no bearing on proceedings.

'I don't know why she is being so vindictive,' said Young. 'I've been on the back foot all the while and it has made me a shell of my old self. While she's had unknown sources prepared to give her money to drag me into court, I can't afford a lawyer. Do you think I want to be sitting in court on my own? I don't have the money to pay for one. It's David versus Goliath.'

However, he took some comfort from the fact that she had already spent £1 million in legal fees. He claimed that, so far, she had been represented by ten law firms over the course of the six-year case – she claimed that this was an exaggeration. Even so, she was embroiled in a High Court battle with solicitors over a £3.5 million no-win, no-fee arrangement to fund investigations into her husband's assets.

The funny thing was, he maintained, he had none. He told the *Daily Mail*'s Angella Johnson: 'Angella, I have no money. I promise you, it's all gone. I want to get back to earning money so I can look after my family but the negative publicity of the many court cases have made it difficult.'

Once again, the outcome of the hearing was inconclusive. The judge ruled that he must produce tax returns and answer a questionnaire on his finances or face jail when he returned to court the following January.

When Young appeared in the High Court in January 2013, he had a new excuse. He said he had failed to produce documents disclosing his assets because he feared that people calling him on his mobile telephone may have been detectives. His wife's 'covert surveillance' of him was making him ill.

'I believe covert surveillance continues on me and it is highly illegal,' he said. 'This is perpetuating my health problems.'

He claimed that his wife was trying to jail him out of 'malice'.

'The motivation is punishment,' he said.

He had 'done everything in [his] power and control' to comply with the orders of the court and asked the judge to give him more time to answer the financial questions posed by Mrs Young. The case was 'incredibly complicated' and he was not represented by a lawyer.

'I was only released from hospital on 10 January [one week earlier] and I was unable to secure the funding which was required to secure the talents of a barrister,' he said.

Again he complained that the situation was that of 'David and Goliath'. He had to defend himself while his wife was represented by a team of lawyers. What's more, 'I have been detained in hospital under the Mental Health Act for fourteen days.'

'Whenever there is a deadline some medical excuse is put forward,' said Edward Fitzgerald, QC, representing Mrs Young. Young's claims of ill health should be treated 'with scepticism' because they often occurred just before court hearings. Mrs Young herself had been seriously ill the previous summer.

Young again complained of harassment. During the case he had been followed by eight detectives working on three shifts, who his wife had hired to record his conversations.

'You can see the level of surveillance I am under,' he told the judge. 'Terrorists are not normally under that amount of surveillance.'

Documents submitted to the court showed that operatives had followed him for up to fourteen hours a day as part of what they were calling 'Operation Lancaster Gate'.

According to the surveillance log, on 2 February 2012, Young could be seen inside his apartment 'wearing a white T-shirt and what appeared to be boxer shorts'. Over the next few days, he was seen taking taxis, eating in restaurants, visiting newsagents and taking bags into a hotel.

On 26 February he was photographed having a drink with his girlfriend, Noelle Reno, at the Pierino Pasta Pizza restaurant in South Kensington. The surveillance log went on: 'Covert video footage is recorded. Unfortunately, the restaurant is busy and very noisy so no audio of SY [Scot Young] and UKF [unknown female] could be understood or picked up.'

Young told the judge that the surveillance was unlawful and had 'perpetuated [his] health problems'. As a result, he had spent two weeks receiving hospital treatment for a mental health condition over Christmas, leaving him unable to gather evidence of his assets.

Asked why he had not accepted a court document that was being served on him, he said he 'did not trust' the official delivering it.

'When you have up to eight individuals following you on three shifts, it's very difficult to know who's a process server and who's a detective employed by my wife,' he said. 'In the condition I am in, paranoia can manifest in many ways, especially when you have eight people following you. I spent fourteen days in hospital under the Mental Health Act. This was at an NHS hospital, not a private one. It was not a nice experience.'

But Edward Fitzgerald QC, for Mrs Young, said he was unconvinced by Mr Young's explanation.

'There is a very deja-vu element to it,' he said, pointing out that Mr Young had made similar excuses before.

'It is a coincidence that at the threat of a committal the same medical excuse is presented in the same terms, by the same hospital,' he said. 'I deal with this with a great deal of scepticism.'

Michelle pointed out that when the court had ordered him

to give full disclosure of his assets back in 2009, he had himself detained in hospital under Section 2 of the Mental Health Act.

'It was a tactic to deceive the court,' Michelle said. 'We've evidence he was busy conducting a million-pound transaction in South America at the time.'

Then, when Mrs Justice Black awarded Michelle £27,500 a month in maintenance, plus a further £6,000 for school fees and rent, Young promptly made himself bankrupt. The court was also told that Mr Young owed £1 million in unpaid maintenance.

Mr Fitzgerald insisted: 'He has never paid a penny. He's been in breach of that order for three-and-a-half years.'

Mrs Young insisted that she had suffered longer than that.

'This has gone on for six years and my daughters and I are not the ones living a life of luxury,' she said. She had no money left and had been funding her case through various 'no win, no fee' agreements.

Seeing things closing in on him, Young begged the judge to give him another twenty-eight days to comply with the disclosure order.

'The difficulty is, I gave you the twenty-eight days on the last occasion,' said Mr Justice Moor. 'All you have done is dodge the question. You are in danger of losing your liberty.'

Once again Mr Fitzgerald said that, while Mr Young was pleading poverty, he seemed to be living a lifestyle 'consistent with considerable wealth' and had been 'going from party to party with champagne glass in his hand and his current girlfriend, some supermodel or other, on his arm, while his wife is being evicted'.

While Mr Young had claimed he was supporting himself by relying on friends and former business associates who paid his rent and living expenses, he had provided no documentation to support this. So far, these gifts Young had received added up to £155,000 in rent and £151,000 in 'other items'.

'There is no documentation in relation to any of that,' Mr Fitzgerald said. 'This is an incredible claim, that all this was made in cash in relation to which there was no documentation at all.'

Indeed, Young admitted that friends had rallied around with £1.5 million, much of which had gone to his wife and daughters. But due to the 'negative publicity' generated by the case, the friends were refusing to provide evidence of the money's origins, he said.

Nor had Young given any explanation as to where the £400 million he had had in 2006 had gone, Mr Fitzgerald said. He had 'flagrantly breached' court orders requiring him to disclose evidence of his assets. He had been ordered to pay his wife and their two daughters £27,500 a month in 2009, but had not paid a penny of the £1 million he owed. What's more, Mr Fitzgerald added: 'He has repeatedly given the court the run-around.'

More than £155 million was moved between accounts linked with Mr Young between 2001 and 2006, Mrs Young's lawyers said. Some £2.4 million was deposited at a bank on the island of Curaçao, in the Dutch Antilles and it was alleged that £224,000 had been withdrawn in 2011 from one company that was supposedly in liquidation in 2009.

Mrs Young was making an 'application to commit' Mr Young to prison for contempt, Mr Fitzgerald said. Young had not complied with court orders to disclose details of finances to Mrs Young and an 'immediate order for committal' was justified.

Young claimed that this was an abuse of process.

'It's clearly vindictive,' he said. 'If she wants answers to questions, how can I give them from prison?'

Mr Justice Moor was not persuaded. He ruled that Young

had failed to obey court orders to provide details of his finances to his wife and was in 'flagrant and deliberate' contempt of court. There had been a 'wholesale failure' to comply with the court orders.

The judge noted, for example, Young completed the sale of a £24 million property in Eaton Square, London, in 2005 and received a ten per cent deposit. The completion statement showed that the money had been transferred to First Curaçao International Bank and Young had been asked to provide evidence he was not the ultimate beneficiary of those funds. However, the judge said his response to this was 'next to useless'. He 'has not got close to answering this question properly' and the excuses he gave for non-compliance were 'absurd'.

Mr Justin Moor said: 'The husband claims he is penniless. The wife contends he is worth up to £400 million but hid all his resources to avoid his obligations to her and their children. I find there has been a flagrant and deliberate contempt over a very long period.'

After this sound reprimand by the judge, Young sat as Mr Justice Moor outlined in minute detail his continuing failure to produce documents or any evidence at all that the capital his wife believes he had hidden – £400 million, maybe as much as £2 billion – had disappeared in a deal he referred to for the first time in court as 'Project Moscow'.

But why had he kept quiet about it for so long? It was over six years since he had told Michelle that he had lost everything on Project Moscow. If he had genuinely lost the money on some failed project in Moscow, surely it would be a simple matter for him to prove it. What was he hiding?

CHAPTER 12

BEHIND BARS

Mr Justice Moor showed no interest in Project Moscow. He was simply fed up with Scot Young's procrastination.

Clearly irritated, the judge noted the next day: 'You have answered "I don't know," or "I don't remember," or, "You will have to ask someone else" to every question.'

He had heard enough and handed down his judgement on both Young's non-disclosure and his failure to comply with the maintenance order – both of which constituted contempt of court.

'I consider both the contempts are serious,' he said. 'They are so serious that a fine – which would be useless as I am satisfied you would not pay – cannot be justified.'

The sentence of six months stood. He banged his gavel and Scot Young was led from the courtroom in handcuffs by a stony-face guard. He was on his way to Belmarsh, a category A prison, usually the home of murderers and terrorists.

'This is a sad day for British justice,' Young said as he left. 'I can't believe I'm locked up with murderers, drug dealers and rapists over a matrimonial matter.'

Prison sentences in divorce cases were rare.

With a knowing twinkle in his eye, he added: 'This makes no sense. All this means is I'll do my time and expunge the contempt order.'

He shot at glassy stare at his wife, then gathered up his Louis Vuitton overnight bag. He gave Noelle Reno one last kiss before he was led away.

'It's not a great day, is it?' she said. 'I didn't expect six months. We were expecting him to be sent down, but it is still very upsetting for me.'

In fact, they had only considered the possibility that he might be sent to prison the previous night. Called in the early evening by journalist from the *Daily Mail*, Young had said there was 'no way I will go to jail'.

He was so sure that he wouldn't be imprisoned that he added airily: 'I think the judge is angry, but I think he'll just give me a slap on the wrist.'

But as the night drew on, his attitude changed.

'We began to think it might happen last night,' said Ms Reno. 'When he came home from court he was quite confident, but at about four in the morning he began making arrangements.'

In the morning, he was still relatively confident.

'I have been inundated with calls from well-wishers,' he told a waiting journalist. 'I've also been talking to my lawyers. I'm bloody exhausted. But I just hope justice will prevail.'

But when he was summoned to hear the judge's verdict, his nerve cracked. Just before he strode through the door of Court 41, he whispered: 'I have a bad feeling about this. I think he is going to send me down.'

This time he was right – and Michelle Young was delighted. Finally, her application to commit had been granted.

'What other choice did I have with someone who is in contempt of court – who is trying to leave me and our two daughters destitute?' she told reporters. Indeed, she was disappointed that he had not been jailed two years earlier.

'It has been a very long, rough ride,' she said. 'I hope I can make a stand for other families who have been left in such dire circumstances after long marriages. We were together eighteen years and wed for twelve. We made this marriage together and I helped with finances, so why should I walk away? This money was made during our time together.'

Asked by the *Glasgow Herald* if she felt relief at the judgement, she said: 'I do, because we have tried every way to get this man to conduct himself [properly] in these proceedings. He has defied every single court order over six-and-a-half years. I have had to secure funding because he personally has hidden the assets unfairly. We started off together and I helped create what we had.'

She added: 'What do you do with someone who hasn't disclosed over six-and-a-half years and left their family completely destitute? It is very abusive. If this sets a precedent today to make other people like Scot Young think again that they can do this to their families then I don't think that is a bad thing. All I want to do is get what I rightly and fairly deserve and to move on. I would hope closure is close now.'

Danae Brook of the *Daily Telegraph* had been on hand again to get the inside story. The day before sentencing, she asked Scot Young: 'Why are you still married?'

'Why indeed?' he replied with a shrug. 'It's in Michelle's hands. We haven't lived together for six years. She has to apply for the divorce and she won't. Why is she trying to commit me to prison? The motivation is punishment, extremely personal to her. Sending me to prison will not advance her position one jot, in fact it will do the opposite.'

Michelle said she was determined to stay married until everything was settled, or at least until she gets the money she feels she is owed. Until then, she was prepared to stick to her guns in a war of attrition.

'My daughters have lost their education,' she said. 'We have moved five times in four years. I share a room with my daughter. We are living in complete limbo. I don't want to go through all this for nothing. I want to see the law changed to protect women like me with children by men who conveniently find they suddenly have no assets when they want to go off with younger women. This isn't the end. There'll be more hearings and the final judgment will come in October.'

Noelle Reno told Ms Banks that she thought Mrs Young was driven either to win the battle or destroy her husband because she became used to an opulent lifestyle, with palatial homes all over the world, funded by Mr Young – and was never self-sufficient.

'She is not just afraid of not having enough money, but also of not having any money,' Ms Reno said.

While Young had described her as 'my girlfriend, my fiancée, my future wife', marriage was not an immediate prospect, she said at the courtroom doors.

'I might be a very, very old woman by then,' Noelle said. 'I put up with all this negativity because I love him and I support him financially and emotionally.'

She admitted lending him money and allowed the court access to her own bank statements.

'Why not?' she asks. 'I have nothing to hide.'

She remained fiercely protective of him, saying he put on a

good face and was too proud to let people know how difficult his life had become; that in court he may appear confident and articulate, but in reality the stress was getting to him. Over Christmas and New Year in St Charles Hospital, an NHS hospital near Ladbroke Grove, he was detained under the Mental Health Act. He was sectioned and put on medication before being allowed out.

Danae Brook was not unsympathetic, but offered another insight into the case outside the courtroom.

'As I left Ms Reno ringing Mr Young's parents and friends on his two mobile phones, it struck me how eerily similar the two woman are,' she wrote. 'Not just their telephones and the constant texting, but the slim frames, tumbling hair, sharp black suits and careful make-up. There might be a gap of nineteen years in age between them, but they both lead their lives in the shadow of the same once-powerful man who could in the end bring them both down.'

A friend of Scot's agreed.

'He has a type,' he said, 'tall, hard-faced blondes.'

Scot Young was not in Belmarsh long and was soon telling the *Mail on Sunday* of his life in Pentonville.

'I'm sharing a cell with a complete stranger and have nothing but a bunk bed and toilet to look at,' he said. 'I'm trying to keep up my spirits over this but it is hard. I never thought in a million years my life would have come to this. Luckily I've managed to lose five pounds by being able to work-out in the prison gym which has saved my sanity.'

Noelle then revealed that she had ended their relationship the month before as there seemed no end to the divorce case.

'I was at breaking point. I said, "I've been waiting around, my life has been on hold, I want to have kids and this is still dragging on. This divorce was meant to be done four years ago!"'

Even so, following the courtroom drama, everything seemed to be on again and she went to visit him in prison.

'It was a bit grim,' she said. 'Young was locked up for almost twenty-three hours a day, and lost twenty-five pounds in weight. But what I love about Scot is that he's a real man. He didn't complain.'

He had lost more weight and it was an emotional experience.

'I was in tears because it is really hard to see Scot in prison,' she said. 'I took him in some fresh clothes which he appreciated. He tells me he is locked up for hours on end and is only allowed out of his cell for an hour's exercise a day. At the moment he says the prison gym is shut so can't use it, which he has been used to, so it is really hard for him. We were allowed a hug, but nothing more. I'm trying to stay strong for him and we are determined prison will not break us.'

She also said that, since he had been jail, his high-profile friends have made themselves scarce.

'Some people have really distanced themselves from him. I am not saying they are cutting Scot out of their life, but the less contact they have with Scot the better,' she said, though she singled out entrepreneur Sir Tom Hunter as the one exception. Nevertheless, the attitude of his associates was understandable.

'The more contact they have – if they help him out with money or are seen with him – Michelle starts thinking "oh that must be because they are hiding all of Scot's billions of dollars",' she said. 'So it is difficult for him to have high-profile friends right now.'

Noelle again dismissed the idea that she and Scot had lived a life of luxury after they had been spotted at high-end restaurants and bars during their three-and-a-half-year relationship.

'Scot's been completely, totally broke for the duration of my entire time with him,' she said, insisting she paid the bill when they went out. And there were other advantages to being a celebrity.

'It might look like we are leading an incredibly glamorous life but a lot of it is complimentary,' she said. 'I get lots of free stuff doing what I do.'

There was no cash under the mattress.

'He told me exactly what everybody else has been told – that he had an earn-out when he sold his tech company,' she said. 'He put the majority of his money into the Moscow property scene and that went awry. Scot was always living a life beyond his means. It is that simple. Like many people, he was never actually living the lifestyle he was seen to be. He didn't really actually have that much money.'

Although she had shed a tear during her visits to Pentonville prison, she said she was now emotionally detached from the legal battle that had 'destroyed so much of my life for so long'.

'It puts a lot of pressure on our relationship, for sure,' she said. 'I am getting to an age now where I don't really want to wait. But I am very strong. Whatever happens we are always going to be best friends, even if he never divorced and we did split up.'

But she still apparently wanted to marry him. When he got out of jail, she said: 'He needs to finish his divorce and get out of bankruptcy.'

Otherwise, she was upbeat. On 9 February, just three weeks after Scot had been sent to prison, she told the *Daily Telegraph*: 'So far, the year has been fine, as work is going great, and Scot and I are going to be fine. I'm going to be so busy with fashion week shows and parties.'

Meanwhile, Mrs Young had Boris Berezovsky in her sights. While Scot Young was in jail, Berezovsky died. The year before, he had lost his suit against Abramovich.

In her ruling, the judge said: 'On my analysis of the entirety of the evidence, I found Mr Berezovsky an unimpressive, and inherently unreliable, witness, who regarded truth as a transitory, flexible concept, which could be moulded to suit his current purposes... I regret to say that the bottom line of my analysis of Mr. Berezovsky's credibility is that he would have said almost anything to support his case.'

During the court case, Berezovsky had accused Abramovich of being a 'gangster'. Abramovich responded by calling Bereszovsky 'something of a megalomaniac'. He was order by the High Court to pay £35 million of Abramovich's legal costs.

Michelle may have drawn inspiration from Berezovsky's own divorce settlement. In 2011, he had divorced his second wife Galina Besharova on the grounds of 'unreasonable behaviour'. After a quickie divorce, they made the settlement behind closed doors. Ms Besharova's lawyer Deborah Levy confirmed that the figure agreed was the 'largest ever' divorce settlement, said to be more than £100 million. Berezovsky married Besharova in 1991 after divorcing his first wife, Nina Korotkova. Besharova was said to have spent only two years of the eighteen-year marriage with the exiled businessman. He was living in Wentworth with Yelena Gorbunova, his partner of fifteen years, and their two children. And his fortune was built up mainly after they had separated. For Michelle, this must have seemed all too easy.

Then he split from Yelena, who had sat beside him in court throughout the Abramovich case. She was claiming that Berezovsky owed her £5 million in compensation over the sale of their £25-million residence in Surrey, along with another £250,000 in legal fees. Though Berezovsky had suffered some reverses, there was a lot to go through. According to *The Sunday Times* Rich List, his net worth was around $900 million. But something else seems to have gone wrong. In the days before his death, he was scrabbling around for money. He was even reported to have sold an Andy Warhol portrait of Lenin for £50,000.

His lawyer, Alexander Dobrovinsky, said: 'He was in a terrible, awful state recently. He had so many debts, he was practically broke.'

One source told *The Times*: 'He had nothing at all left, nothing. He couldn't even pay for lunch.'

He claimed that he was £200 million in debt – not a billionaire, but 'the poorest man in the world'.

Former rival Boris Nemstov said: 'He lost money, he lost to Abramovich and he lost his wife... he not only suffered financially but personally.'

One close friend confirmed Berezovsky had been taking antidepressants and had checked into the Priory clinic briefly to be treated for depression.

'He was very, very low,' the friend said. 'He talked about suicide. He would say to me: "It's all over, it's all finished, there's no point in anything – the best thing that could happen to me is that I have a heart attack."'

But the friend did not take this seriously.

'I still don't believe he had the courage to take his own life,' he said. 'He loved life too much.'

On 23 March 2013, Berezovsky's body was found in the bathroom at his home at Sunninghill near Ascot, Berkshire. His bodyguard called the police, who sent officers trained in handling chemical, biological and nuclear material. Detectives created a two-mile cordon around the mansion while specialist officers wearing protective clothing examined the scene. Initially, they thought that Berezovsky might have been poisoned by a radioactive substance like Litvinenko, but no nuclear contamination was found.

It then emerged that the bathroom door was locked from the inside. The police conducted a fingertip search of the surroundings and treated the death as 'unexplained', perhaps linked to attacks on other prominent Russians living in Britain. However, they found no evidence to suggest that a third party had been involved.

The historian Dr Yuri Felshinsky did not believe that his friend had killed himself. Although he had financial difficulties, he was looking forward to testifying at the inquest into Litvinenko's death which, the previous week, had been postponed until October.

'When we recently spoke for the last time, Boris was looking to the future and did not seem to be suicidal,' said Dr Felshtinsky. 'We spoke about his daughter. Boris feared for his safety and understood that the Kremlin aimed to destroy him as an example for anyone else who opposed Putin. Boris understood the Kremlin mindset better than anyone. He had personal security but it was not of the kind he'd had when he lived in Russia.'

In exile in the US, Dr Felshtinsky thought he knew where to put the blame.

'Putin was dealing with Boris in the way he deals with all his enemies,' he said. 'Boris was a fighter and suicide was not in his DNA.'

Russian opposition activist Sergei Parkhomenko, talking to liberal radio station Ekho Moskvy about Berezovsky's differences with Putin, said: 'We were talking once and we turned to the strange topic of health and illness. He told me: "My health is yet another weapon. Who dies first, loses. And I never lose".'

The conclusion was clear.

'He didn't seem like a potential suicide,' Parkhomenko added.

BEHIND BARS

A spokesman for Putin, Dmitry Peskov, acknowledged that Berezovsky had been an enemy.

'We know for certain that he spared no expense in support of processes, within Russia and beyond, that could be said to have been directed against Russia and Putin,' Peskov said. 'He definitely was Putin's opponent, and unfortunately not only his political opponent, but most likely in other dimensions as well.'

However, Peskov said that Berezovsky had written a personal letter to the Russian president two months earilier, asking for forgiveness.

'Boris Berezovsky passed a letter personally written by him,' Peskov said. 'He admitted that he made lots of mistakes and asked Vladimir Putin to forgive him. He asked Putin for a chance to come back to Russia.'

Sixty-seven-year-old Berezovsky's twenty-three-year-old girlfriend Katerina Sabirova, a model, confirmed that he had sent the letter.

'I said that they will publish it and you will look bad. And that it won't help,' she said. 'He answered that it was all the same to him, that in any case all sins were blamed on him and that this was his only chance.'

Berezovsky was desperate to go back to Russia without facing a long jail sentence.

'He said that he wasn't bothered how it would look,' she said. 'The main thing was that he needed to return home... I saw the draft text. He read it to me. He expressed his apologies and asked about the possibility of returning home. He caved in.'

According to the newspaper *Vedomosti* and the Russian news channel TV Rain, it was Abramovich who brought the letter to Moscow. A spokesman for Abramovich refused to comment, saying: 'This is a personal matter.'

Asked if she believed the businessman could have committed suicide, Ms Sabirova answered: 'No. He was saying, "Imagine, if I am no more. All their problems will disappear." But that wasn't a guide to action.'

Indeed, the following Monday, they had agreed to meet in Tel Aviv for a two-week holiday in Eilat. She already had her ticket. Friends confirmed that they had been seeing each other for some time. She said that she had often stayed on his Wentworth Park Estate, before he had had to sell it.

She had noticed a change in him recently though.

'He was smoking a lot, sometimes several packs a day,' she said. 'He ate very little and by the time of our last meeting he had got very thin.'

She said that Berezovsky had asked her to bring Chinese herbal medicines from Moscow, which he made into a soup to help him overcome insomnia.

In the High Court, just two days after Berezovsky had died, Mrs Young's new barrister Tosin Oguntayo told Mr Justice Moor: 'One of the parties which she feels has been hiding funds for Mr Young was the late Mr Boris Berezovsky.'

The finger had been pointed by a forensic accountant working for Mrs Young. According to Mr Ogunayo, he had found significant evidence to show Mr Young was not insolvent. Young was not at the hearing. He was not represented and was unavailable for comment.

CHAPTER 13

TREASURE ISLANDS

Data from the British Virgin Islands leaked to the Washington based International Consortium of Investigative Journalists showed that Scot Young had used a network of off-shore companies to hold his assets during his multi-million pound divorce battle. The data had come from a hard drive sent to the ICIJ by post, showing that some £21 trillion was stashed in secret accounts. It was the latest of a series of leaks of client information that rocked off-shore centres.

'I find it disgraceful the amount of money that has been allowed to be hidden off-shore, and that it is legal to put assets out of reach in cases like mine,' said Michelle Young. 'Obviously this accelerates my case. I will now be calling all of the people named in this document to the High Court.'

The disk revealed some of the dealings of lawyer Stephen Jones, the owner of off-shore specialist Jirehouse Capital. He was the lawyer who had called Mrs Young in March 2006 to tell her that her husband had lost all his money and had checked into the Priory – though when she checked later she found there was no record of his admission. Jones did not dispute making the call, but would not reveal the contents as they were 'subject to legal professional privilege held by our clients'.

In 2005, as his marriage deteriorated, Young had joined forces with Russian businessman Ruslan Fomichev, formerly Berezovsky's business partner, to invest in a £65-million deal to redevelop the site of a former paint factory in Moscow with shops and offices. Fomichev sold him a half share in an off-shore company in Cyprus called Parasol Participations Ltd, which controlled the planned redevelopment. Their secret deal involved twelve obscure companies and trusts in Cyprus, Russia, Lichtenstein and the British Virgin Islands.

On 28 March 2006, Young signed a power of attorney giving Jones control of 'interests held by me in Parasol Participations'. This gave Jones the authority to transfer Young's interests to Solar Breeze Ltd and five other companies all registered in the British Virgin Islands.

A week later, at a meeting held in Monaco, Jones took control of these companies. The following morning, the companies and shares were shifted to the tiny Caribbean island of Nevis. Jones then established a new Nevis-based trust, the SY Refinance Foundation, to 'restructure' Young's financial affairs. Meanwhile, Young was claiming that he had lost all his money when 'Project Moscow' collapsed. All this took place before Mrs Young had obtained a global freezing order on all her husband's assets in June 2007.

In May 2009, Young had already been warned by a judge that he faced imprisonment if he did not do his utmost to reveal full details of his finances. According to the documents leaked to the ICIJ, two days later, agents appointed by Young sought to merge the six companies that controlled his half share in Project Moscow. The consolidation went ahead on 17 August 2009. The sole share in the new company, Solar Breeze (Consolidated) Limited, was issued to Stephen Jones's company Jirehouse Fiduciaries Nominees of Nevis.

With the divorce battle raging, Jirehouse Fiduciaries Nominees of Nevis took full ownership of Parasol Participations of Cyprus on 4 July 2012. As a result, Jones's clients, who included Young, owned all of the potentially lucrative Moscow development.

Jones denied fronting for the jailed tycoon. He told the *Guardian*: 'We only ever acted on behalf of various creditors – and upon the express instructions of those creditors – of Mr and Mrs Young and have never acted for Mr or Mrs Young or represented any of their respective interests.'

Though the sums seemed substantial enough, Young was just small-fry caught in the ICIJ leak. Others include French President Francois Hollande's campaign treasurer Jean-Jacques Augier, who was forced to reveal the identity of his mysterious Chinese partner, Xi Shu; Bayartsogt Sangajav, the former finance minister of cash-strapped Mongolia who kept £1 million off-shore; the president of Azerbaijan Ilham Aliyev and his two daughters; Olga Shuvalova, the wife of Russia's deputy prime minister; Tony Merchant, the husband of a Canadian senator, who deposited $800,000 in an off-shore trust; Maria Imelda Marcos Manotoc, eldest daughter of former President Ferdinand Marcos, now a provincial governor in the Philippines; Baroness Carmen Thyssen-Bornemisza, Spain's wealthiest art collector who used off-shore companies to buy pictures; and Denise Rich, ex-wife of notorious oil trader Marc Rich, who was controversially pardoned by President Clinton on tax evasion charges. More than a million companies and trusts were incorporated in the Caribbean micro-state, which thought to conceal more than $20 trillion.

Finally, Michelle Young had solid evidence about where her husband's missing millions had gone.

'His dishonesty is staggering,' she said. 'He has lied to me and is clearly without regard for the British justice system. This is the proof, if it were even needed, that he has no respect for the law whatsoever. People like Scot, people with wealth and power, believe that the rules do not apply to them. He has broken my global freezing order, something that I knew he had done but now finally there is proof.'

Not only did she threaten to call all the people listed, she said she would be gunning for others involved as well. Some of them were big players and not the sort of people who wanted to be messed with.

'Of course I'm going to take this to court,' she told the *Glasgow Herald*. 'And obviously the next ones to be pursued will be all the third parties involved. This is a criminal conspiracy. The battle is a lot bigger than Scot Young. Big business is behind this. There are major banks involved, which will all be disclosed in the next couple of months within the court room.'

Even though the evidence was piling up against him, just two weeks later, Scot Young was released from jail, complaining about being locked up with 'murderers, drug dealers and rapists'. He walked to freedom with his Louis Vuitton bag slung over his shoulder and a cigarette in his hand, having served just three months of his six-month sentence.

Noelle was waiting for him. The pair went straight out for an expensive lunch. Later he was seen at an art exhibition in Soho with Noelle. But she would spend just three days with him before jetting off to Monaco, where she was to be the star guest at the Style Lab's party for nightclub Zelo and attend the Monte Carlo Rolex Masters tennis event.

'She has missed Scot but she can't wait for some sunshine in Monaco,' said a friend.

When she got back, she was seen at a gala dinner for Denise Rich's Gabrielle's Angel Foundation in Battersea Power Station.

'It's great to have Scot back,' she told a gossip columnist. 'He is really well. Everything has gone back to how it was; we're really happy.'

She was also working on a fashion range for a well-known brand and was planning her own collection. And plainly she and Scot had kissed and made up. A month later, it was clear they were an item again.

'He's got a hold on me, I don't know what else to say,' she said.

Noelle's ambition to wed came one step closer later that month when Michelle Young obtained a ninety-second 'quickie divorce', citing 'abusive behaviour'. In legal papers, she claimed: 'I suffered insomnia, as did the children, as a consequence of the respondent's abusive behaviour.'

However, she said she would not agree to the divorce being made absolute, allowing her ex-husband to remarry, until the financial arrangements have been completed.

Scot did not contest the quickie divorce, but was ordered to pay costs – though he claimed he could not afford to.

'I am technically insolvent, but if my financial position changes I am happy to pay,' he maintained.

But Michelle took no prisoners. Immediately she began pushing for another court order to have her errant husband thrown back in jail. She assembled a new legal team 'who have the expertise to deal with this'.

'He's still in contempt of court,' she said. 'How can the

justice system let him take one step out of prison without him disclosing the whereabouts of the £400 million?'

She thought he should have stayed in the prison until he purged his contempt.

'It's outrageous that he's out celebrating,' she said.

But Mrs Young would not have long to wait. Scheduling a final showdown to get to the bottom of Mr Young's finances in October 2013, Mr Justice Moor said: 'Let's not beat about the bush. Mrs Young's case is that his friends are a front for [Mr Young's] wealth... I want to hear from these people.'

The judge was scathing about the alleged role of his illustrious business associates.

'It is absurd to say that these friends are prepared to support him financially to such a huge extent but that not one of them is prepared to produce any documentary evidence that the money came from them,' he said. 'There is no evidence he has tried to obtain such information from them. He knew what was required. I conclude he has deliberately failed to comply.'

But did Mr Young's friends want to be heard from? Sir Philip Green was puzzled by the judge's remarks, insisting that everything he had done for the Youngs was above board. He told *The Independent*: 'I paid UK cheques from my bank account.'

Asked why Young had failed to produce documentary evidence to support this, he replied: 'I don't know. I don't want to get involved in this. I don't know what this has to do with me. I'm just telling you categorically that any money I may have paid came from my own personal UK bank account. End of conversation.'

A spokesman for Sir Tom Hunter said: 'Our support for the family is a matter of public record. Clearly if asked by the courts Tom would of course give evidence on this matter.'

Unperturbed by the fact that her fiancé may be going back

to jail, Ms Reno announced her forthcoming nuptials in the *Daily Telegraph* – but it would not be on her reality-TV show *Ladies of London*.

'We're hoping to get married next year,' she told the newspaper. 'I wouldn't have the wedding on the show because it's private.'

They had already had their reconciliation in front of the cameras. Noelle complained that the experience was 'massively intrusive'. But those were the rules of the game in reality TV.

'If there's a conversation you have off-camera, you have to have it again on-camera,' she said, 'and if you're not being honest it comes across.'

Meanwhile, the *Independent* was hard at work unearthing more pecuniary peculiarities about the case. There was a mysterious bank account still held by HBOS – Halifax Bank of Scotland – after the voluntary liquidation of a company linked to Young. The £1.1 million generated by the liquidation of the firm was unaccounted for. Another £300,000 produced during the wind-up of the company was held by the bank for five years. Then there was £100,000 sent to a law firm that had represented Mr Young – eighteen months after he was officially declared bankrupt. The bank maintained the transfer was not related to him though.

There were more irregularities concerning the bank. In a sworn affidavit outlining his financial position, Young claimed that, at the height of his wealth, HBOS had provided him with mortgages totalling £29 million to buy six luxury properties in Oxfordshire, London and Miami between 2001 and 2005. Young then told the High Court that these properties – including Wootton Place – were repossessed by the bank and sold at a profit of over £17 million. He failed to explain how this had not cleared the £3 million he owed the bank.

Then there was the mystery of Dione House, the headquarters of his chip-and-pin company in High Wycombe, Buckinghashire, which was just half-an-hour's drive away from his home in Oxfordshire. A week before he bought Wootton Place, Dione House was sold to Condor Corporate Services Ltd. Young's business associate Gwilym Davies was a director of the company when it went into voluntary liquidation in late 2006, six months after Young claimed to have gone bust.

Dione House was sold in December 2006 for £6.25 million, some £324,550 of which was transferred into an 'internal' account opened at HBOS that month, marked 're Condor Corporate Services', said to be 'under the control of the bank', according to leaked documents obtained by the *Independent*. The sum was listed as 'redemption fees' and 'XS redemption funds' on bank statements. HBOS confirmed that it related to 'the sale of a property'.

But this money does not appear as part of the liquidation. The chairman's statement lodged at Companies House included an £80,000 early redemption fee. However, the *Independent*'s analysis of the company's statements revealed a surplus of £1.1 million unaccounted for.

Questioned by the newspaper about the disparity between the £324,550 redemption fees logged in the internal HBOS bank account and the £80,000 redemption charge declared to Companies House, a spokesman for the bank said: 'We do not intend to comment on confidential matters.'

The money remained in the account, untouched for five years until, in September 2011 – eight months after Young was declared bankrupt –£100,000 was paid to a law firm that had been representing him in the divorce proceedings.

This payment, the bank said, was made on behalf of a former director of Condor Corporate Services who had been in dispute with the liquidator. Young told the same story to the High Court. The account related to a disagreement between Mr Davies and the liquidator, he said, but he could not go into details due to a confidentially agreement he had entered into when the conflict was resolved.

Again, HBOS told the *Independent* that it could not comment due to client confidentiality, and it would not explain how there could be a client when the account was internal and 'under the bank's control'. The £225,000 remaining in the account after the £100,000 had been paid was then was paid back to HBOS in 'exit fees'.

When asked who controlled the bank account and who authorised the payment to Young's law firm eighteen months after he went bankrupt, a Bank of Scotland spokesperson told the *Independent*: 'This was an internal account opened by the Bank, to which the customer had no access. Due to issues of customer confidentiality, we are unable to provide you with any further information on this account.'

Accountants Grant Thorton Partners, who had been appointed by HMRC to look into Scot Young's affairs, investigated Condor Corporate Services and found nothing improper.

Senior partner David Ingram, the court-appointed trustee, said: 'I've had discussions with those people and what I have undertaken has left me with the impression that there is no smoking gun. I'm aware that there are some confidentialities and I am not going to upset that confidentiality agreement.'

However, Ingram, who also worked regularly for the Serious Fraud Office, said that his investigations had been hampered when Young became ill. This was the same difficulty the High Court had when trying to force Young to come clean about his financial affairs.

Mrs Young had some fresh information too. She had

uncovered emails that showed her husband, while under the six-month suspended sentence handed down in June 2009, was 'clearly continuing in business' and conducting off-shore deals, particularly in the Isle of Man. Her lawyers also alleged that he had faked illness in order to 'manipulate the court system'.

Coincidentally, Grant Thornton was also involved in unravelling the estate of the late Boris Berezovsky. They told the High Court that the oligarch did not leave enough to pay off debts, including a huge potential liability of £100 million to HMRC. But lawyers for the Berezovsky family insisted that Grant Thornton had failed to identify numerous assets.

'The work simply hasn't been done,' said Henry Legge, QC, a barrister for Berezovsky's former partner, Yelena Gorbunova.

CHAPTER 14

SHOWDOWN IN THE COURTROOM

For some time, Mr Young had been representing himself. But as the final four-week courtroom showdown approached – where Sir Philip Green, Richard Caring, Harold Tillman and Sir Tom Hunter were likely to be called – he managed to engage the services of Raymond Tooth, one of Britain's most expensive divorce lawyers, who had represented Sadie Frost in her battle with Jude Law and Irina Abramovich, the ex-wife of the owner of Chelsea Football Club. She had won an estimated £150 million in a quickie divorce in 2007. Irina, mother of Abramovich's five children, was his second wife. Olga, his first wife, said he left her with a two-bedroom flat in Moscow and just enough money to live on for two years when they split in 1989. After sixteen years of marriage, fifty-one-year-old Roman swapped forty-six-year-old Irina for twenty-five-year-old Daria 'Dasha' Zhukova, daughter of another oligarch.

Asked how he was able to represent a bankrupt, a spokesperson for Tooth said: 'We do not discuss any matters regarding the affairs of clients with investigating reporters. Furthermore, you should not assume that we act for Mr Young. You must be aware of the duty of confidentiality.'

In court, Young sought to protect his wealthy friends. Justin Warshaw, also acting for him, argued his 'friends and sponsors' had provided witness statements and their evidence should not be challenged by Mrs Young.

Mr Justice Moor said that would amount to a 'ridiculous situation'. He added: 'I consider it almost inconceivable that she would not be able to challenge them... If these people are saying that they funded Mr Young then she is entitled to cross-examine them.'

However, Young found he had a surprise ally. When Mrs Young sought to have her ex-husband's bankruptcy annulled, she found herself challenged by HM Revenue & Customs.

Christopher Buckley, for HMRC, said: 'We will be opposing this very vigorously.'

Again Mr Justice Moor was puzzled.

'Don't they want to get their money?' he asked. 'I would have thought HMRC, as a creditor, would be absolutely delighted?'

Mrs Young then stood up in court and yelled 'Corporate corruption!' – before being told to be quiet by her lawyer. In its defence, HMRC issued a statement, saying: 'HMRC maintains the highest standards of honesty and integrity at all times in its dealings with all its customers. We strongly reject any comments suggesting otherwise.'

Once the financial hearings proper got underway, Mrs Young lowered her sights and said that she would settle for a mere £300 million – knocking £100 million off her previous demand – even though she continued to maintain that her husband was worth 'a few billion at least'. She also wanted him to cover her legal expenses. Plainly, she thought her husband was in the oligarch's league.

Later, Mrs Young's barrister Rex Howling, QC, told the court that her estranged husband had 'previously offered, on an open basis, to settle her claim for £300 million' years after he claimed to have lost all his money.

To start with, she said needed a £25 million home in Belgravia.

'It's a nice area. It's very safe,' she said. 'This case is not about means. It's about quality.'

The case was like no other in the family division of the High Court, she maintained. 'Vast amounts of assets have been concealed. It was a very long marriage. My children and I should be entitled to a fair share of those assets... We had vast estates. We had staff. We had a very luxury lifestyle. We had a chandelier in our drawing room. The other chandelier sits in the White House. They were valuable assets.'

There were other valuable antiques.

'I paid £10,000 for a beautiful piece of furniture around fifteen or eighteen years ago,' she said. 'It was a beautiful side piece. I bought that at Sotheby's.'

Mrs Young said they had moved house a number of times and the profit on one house was '£10million'.

She claimed her ex-husband would spend up to £5,000 in restaurants, paid £2 million to £4 million for 'a flash gin-palace, Sunseeker-type boat' and had talked about buying a 'very expensive helicopter' to fly between a home near Oxford and London. They went on three or four foreign holidays each year, staying in villas and presidential suites.

Her jewellery, which Young had said cost 'a million pounds', was auctioned at Sotheby's for between £160,000 and £180,000 to pay for her rent and legal fees. The collection included a diamond necklace, diamond bracelet and two diamond rings.

She told the judge: 'My husband has never produced a shred of real evidence about where one asset has gone to.' She accused him of being 'incredibly' secretive about finance and accused him of hiding his 'vast fortune' off-shore.

He dealt in property, but had also told her father that he had made 'vast money on telecommunications'. It was all hidden in off-shore accounts.

'He was constantly on the phone to his high-profile friends and advisers talking about multi-million-pound deals,' she said. 'If I heard it... he'd quickly run off or jump out of the Phantom or Ferrari so I couldn't hear. I wasn't made aware of very much regarding the business side.'

And she knew where to point the finger.

'There was a vast fortune hidden,' she said. 'He used off-shore vehicles and many advisers and accountants to layer these assets. This has dragged through the courts for seven years mostly because of my husband's lack of disclosure and playing the system.'

Rolling his eyes, Mr Young asked the judge: 'Is this kind of ranting allowed?'

Plainly the hearings had got off to a bad start. But they were never going to be amicable and Mr Justice Moor explained his task in these hearings to the court.

'I have to decide on the balance of probabilities how much Mr Young is worth,' he said.

This was not going to be easy. Mr Howling, for Mrs Young, said: 'Many witnesses are expressing a reluctance to come to court and several, particularly those with a high media profile, appear to be conveniently out of the jurisdiction for the whole of the trial window.'

Young's friends and associates had done a runner.

Mr Howling told the judge that Harold Tillman, who had been served with a witness summons, had 'made it clear that he will be outside of the jurisdiction' for the entire four-week hearing and would be unavailable to give evidence. The court was also told that Sir Philip Green had declined to give evidence under oath on Mr Young's behalf. Mrs Young's lawyers said the billionaire Topshop owner made two 'very forceful telephone calls' saying he would not appear in the witness box.

'On both occasions he was saying, in no uncertain terms, "I am not coming".'

Mr Justice Moor intervened, saying: 'If you need them, tell us, and we will get them here.'

Young protested: 'This is causing me considerable anguish. Philip Green has a certain reluctance to come to court because of the media circus. I spoke to Sir Philip last week. He said: "I don't know why you are getting involved, leave it to me".'

Mrs Young claimed it was not going to be possible to find out how much her ex-husband was worth unless these witnesses were called because of all the shady deals they were involved in. One deal alone involving Mr Young, Sir Philip and Sir Tom had earned them £80 million, which was then transferred into shares in the name of Sir Philip's wife, Tina Green.

The case centred on a £400 million schedule of assets that Mr Young was alleged to have lodged with the leading law firm Fox Williams in 2006. Details had been recovered from the hard drive of a wiped laptop Mr Young had given their eldest daughter to do her homework in 2008 by forensic investigators instructed by Mrs Young.

She said she had obtained further documents through search-and-seize orders that suggested Mr Young was involved in the flotation of multibillion-pound technology companies. One of them was a hand-written note seized from Mr Young's London hotel room in 2012, suggesting he was involved a major deal with Sean Parker, one of the founding investors of Facebook.

First of all, Mrs Young wanted his bankruptcy overturned.

'I believe all the debts are fictitious and it's all part of the restructuring of his assets,' she said.

Asked by Mr Young how he had hidden all his wealth, she said: 'You have advisers at the Bank of Scotland and law firms, who move assets from A to B.'

She also accused her ex-husband of operating a 'golden handcuffs' policy that, through 'bribery and corruption', had managed to prevent third parties from disclosing their knowledge of his hidden wealth held in up to twenty-five jurisdictions around the world.

'I need a huge lump-sum order in order to go and collect these assets that belong to me and my children,' she told the judge.

Questioning American financial investigator L. Burke Files, president of the investigative firm Financial Examinations &Evaluations based in Arizona, Mr Howling said there appeared to be occasions where assets or shares had been transferred by Mr Young, then later appeared in the name of his lieutenants. Mr Files agreed.

Asked what he thought of Mr Young's business empire Mr Files said many of the properties were purchased through a holding company whose shares were later sold.

'In many cases the properties borrowed money... and then would be sold,' he said. 'Often the debtors appear to be beneficially owned – either directly or indirectly – by Mr Young.'

Mr Files told the court that there was a 'double or second layering of debt' on many of the tycoon's assets.

'Mr Young was borrowing from Mr Young to lend to Mr

Young to hide the assets,' Files said. 'If the money came from somewhere it has to be deployed somewhere else. It can't just evaporate.'

Mr Files told the court how Mr Young would also briefly transfer assets to his business associates and then move them back to his 'first lieutenant' – his associate Gwilym Davies. Mr Howling said Davies was a director of Milvus Ventures Ltd and read out an attendance note referring to the company that said: 'Scot can put income through this.'

Mr Howling asked if this meant the company was an 'income stream' for Mr Young. Mr Files replied: 'Yes it does.'

Taking the stand, Davies admitted that his boss was 'quite secretive' and would 'keep the bigger things to himself'. When he told the court that his salary from Mr Young was £120,000 a year, Mrs Young audibly scoffed.

'The various schedules suggest that Mr Young could have been telling his advisers that he was worth as much as £500 million in 2005/06,' Mr Howling told the judge. 'Mr Young has resolutely failed to provide evidence of where his money has gone. Mrs Young asserts that Mr Young has transferred his beneficial interest in the majority of his assets to a number of closely allied third parties.'

The court also heard that Hexagon Registrars Ltd, registered at the address of Mr Young's commercial law firm Fox Williams, purchased another company 'on trust for Scot'.

Mr Files also said he had traced other business dealings by Mr Young through 'dollar transactions in New York', but there were problems.

'When I tried to download them the thousands of documents were so vast that it crashed several computers,' he said

Mr Howling also gave the court a list of holdings owned by Mr Young and registered in Jersey which the tycoon had never disclosed. These showed he once had £17 million of interests in companies such as Woolworths and Marks and Spencer.

The same month as Young said he lost all his money, he owned 3.1 million shares in O_2 worth more than £6 million. This money was then used to buy the waterfront property in the affluent Miami suburb of Coconut Grove. The purchase was made through a company called Greenfield Horizons in the British Virgin Islands.

The role of the Bank of Scotland – HBOS – was also raised in court as it was listed as a major creditor of Mr Young. Mr Howling said that Mr Young once gave HBOS an 'unsupported personal guarantee' of £3 million. He asked Mr Files: 'How likely is it that a corporation the size of HBOS would take an unsecured guarantee?'

But the money was there. Mr Files said that Mr Young had simply 'restructured his empire' by 'moving assets around'.

'This is not unusual in the least bit,' Files told the court. 'The money is a tool. It goes back into the system to be used. The velocity of the money circulation can only be guessed.'

Concerning the hand-written note seized from Mr Young's hotel room, Mr Files said: 'I have seen a Post-it note talking about a $4.5 billion [£2.8 billion] profit in Facebook.'

He read out an email written by a man called Chris Dunhill, dated October 2011, that said Mr Young was a 'good friend of [Simon] Cowell, [Sir Philip] Green and [Boris] Berezovsky'. It went on to refer to a man called George Constantine, who Dunhill said 'looks after Scot's properties which of course he doesn't have technically any more'. Mr Files said the email 'goes to the foundation of the incongruities' he dealt with in coming to the conclusion that Mr Young was still a very wealthy man.

Files also confirmed that one of Mr Young's companies had

an 'open and active bank account in 2011' – eig.
after the tycoon was declared bankrupt and two yea
company was liquidated.

an 'open and active bank account in 2011' – eighteen months after the tycoon was declared bankrupt and two years after the company was liquidated.

The American investigator said: 'That hit me like a dead cat buying groceries. It suggests that he is using that bank account to secrete money from his creditors.'

Under cross-examination, Young asked Files if he agreed with his claim that Bank of Scotland had repossessed all his properties. Files replied: 'No, I don't agree at all.'

Mr Young then turned to the judge and denied he was 'in cahoots' with the bank, which itself had to be bailed out with £20 billion of taxpayers' money in 2008.

Later, Files was asked about a £6 million beachfront property in Miami that Young claimed had been repossessed by HBOS.

Files replied: 'That is not correct... The amount that was not paid to the Bank of Scotland was routed through an American law firm to the Poju Zabludowicz Trust and £750,000 was paid back to Mr Young.'

Zabludowicz, of course, was Young's partner in Dione, a chip-and-pin technology company, who, by then, had a good friend in Downing Street.

Mr Justice Moor was also told that private investigators watching Mr Young had noticed that he 'spent a lot of time hanging off mobile phones'. This was where he did his business.

'Scot spends a huge amount of time on the phone,' said Ms Reno. 'He's not very good at typing e-mails. He talks on the phone in an old-fashioned sort of way. He's bored.'

She insisted that he had not been 'wheeling and dealing', but talking to 'his friends'.

'Nobody wants to do business with Scot right now,' she said.

Noelle felt at home in the courtroom. Her father was a retired lawyer and federal prosecutor.

'I know that he wants to support his daughters,' she told the judge. 'It kills him that he can't. And he wants to support Michelle.'

Asked why he 'can't go and get a job in Tesco?' Ms Reno replied: 'Even Tesco probably wouldn't want to get involved.'

Their rent was around £4,000 a month but one of Mr Young's friends 'named Nick' paid it, she said. She lent Scot cash and picked up household expenses.

'I am not supporting him,' she told the court. 'I have loaned him some money. I pay the utility bills. I pay for the Tesco shopping.'

She denied being a 'cash courier' for the tycoon. But Mr Howling said she had been observed by private investigators withdrawing £25,000 in cash from her own bank account in July 2011 and handing it to Young, who appeared to be in an 'agitated state'. When asked why, she said: 'Maybe he had an arrangement with the person to pay them cash,' said Miss Reno. 'Maybe he didn't want me to know who the person was.'

Mr Howling asked why someone who was bankrupt would owe such a sum and suggested Miss Reno was being 'misleading'.

'I am absolutely not misleading you,' she said. 'I try to get involved as little as possible. I am being persecuted for helping someone. I have my own problems. I'm being dragged into this. I don't want to know.'

The court also heard of a note written to Mr Young by her brother, 'Chip', that was seized from her flat in another court-approved raid. It read: 'Thank you for picking up all the cheques, cab rides, bar tabs and everything else.' Ms Reno said her brother was only talking of 'a couple of hundred pounds'.

As the case was all about money, the judge began to worry about how much it was costing. Mr Young was claiming penury, while Mrs Young was borrowing up to the eyeballs. Concerning their finances, Mr Justice Moor said: 'I have no doubt I am going to be saying something about the costs in this case. It has concerned me, the amount of costs being run up in this case.'

More witness were called to testify to Mr Young's apparent wealth.

Young's friend and business associate Ben Anderson told the court: 'I always thought he was very, very wealthy and was shocked when the crash came in 2006.'

In a written statement, paparazzo Dennis Gill said that Young had offered him £150 to destroy the photograph of the supposedly penniless tycoon walking into London restaurant Nobu in October 2009. Apparently, there was no end to Young's generosity.

'He said he would pay me £2,000 in cash tax-free if I would follow his wife on Friday taking a video and photos of whom she was with,' Gill said in the sworn affidavit. 'I said, "OK sure" and he said he would call me. Scot then said, "Between me and you mate, I offered her £27 million and she refused it, only a greedy cow would refuse that." He then said, "What greedy cow would refuse that?" I said that was not for me to say. He told me to keep it under my hat and not to tell anyone.

'He continued chatting and told me that he pays for everything in cash so that his wife cannot keep track of what he is spending.'

Young denied making these remarks and denied making the offer of £27 million to his wife.

In court, Gill appeared to distance himself from the statement which had been made four years before, telling the court of his increasing deafness.

'To the best of my knowledge, I did hear him say that, but I could have misinterpreted, because of my ears,' he said. 'It could have been wrong, it could have been right.'

However, after his cross-examination continued, he insisted that he was 'a thousand per cent sure' that Mr Young had said the things attributed to him.

Gill had known the couple from his work in London and said that both had offered to pay him to follow the other. He also said Mrs Young told him she lived in a bedsit, relying on food hand-outs and charity shops, but he had seen her at many exclusive nightclubs and at the Dorchester Hotel with actress and TV presenter Donna Air, who was dating the Duchess of Cambridge's brother.

'How can she afford to go to one of these places, and she is telling me she's broke?' Gill said.

Young's former solicitor Stanley Beller was also called. He said that Young had once boasted he had a collection of over forty watches worth £2 million and had been involved in a deal to buy the Sultan of Brunei's car collection. Young, he said, had once walked out of his office with £13 million of share certificates, taken from his safe, in March 2006 – the month Young claimed to have become 'hopelessly insolvent'. This effectively ruined him, Beller said.

While Young always denied owning shares in the telecoms giant O_2, Beller read a letter from 2006 instructing the lawyer to sell 'my portfolio' of 3.1 million shares 'in the capital of O_2' worth more than £6 million. It was signed by Mr Young.

On another occasion a transaction had been made via a 'holdall full of cash'. According to Beller, Young handed Harvey Lawrence, one of his creditors, £4 million in cash in 2008, two years after the tycoon claimed to have lost all his money.

Young, who had once been a guest at the bar mitzvah of Mr Beller's son, protested Beller was lying, but Beller told the judge: 'I am not going to be called a liar by this cheat.'

CHAPTER 15

PROJECT MARRIAGE WALK

In court, Mrs Young's barrister, Rex Howling QC, asked Mr
Young for an explanation of 'Project Marriage Walk'. It was
one of a number of projects listed in documents belonging
to Mr Young that his ex-wife had gone through. The name
suggested it 'may have been a plan to exit your marriage'.

'It is not unreasonable that you may have had in place an
exit strategy as early as 2002?' Mr Howling asked.

Young said he could not recall what the project was.

'I strongly refute that this was me planning to exit my
marriage,' he added, describing the allegation as 'ridiculous'.

Plainly to leave his wife and start again with someone
else was going to be expensive. Some of his friends had been
through it and it had cost them millions. But somehow all the
money Young had had when he was married had disappeared.
Yet somehow, though bankrupt, Young managed to continue
living like a wealthy man, supposedly on the handouts of

friends. The clear implication was that Project Marriage Walk was a way to hide his money off-shore and behind a screen of shell companies and have the money he needed to maintain his lifestyle channelled back to him through friends and associates.

That way Young could continue to claim that he was penniless and he insisted that the £4,000-a-month rent on the central London flat where he lived with Noelle Reno was paid by businessman Nick Alexander, who was 'a very good friend'.

'I very much enjoy living in the West End,' he said.

Other friends had given him large amounts of cash to survive.

Mr Howling suggested that Young could live in a cheaper apartment and give money to his wife.

'I don't speak to my wife,' Young said. 'The people who give me money would certainly not give me money to give to my wife after what she has done in the press by selling stories, inaccurate stories. A lot of people are very unhappy with my wife.'

So any sort of negotiation was out of the question and, at the moment, he was not in a position to help his family.

'I am basically not the man I was,' he admitted. 'I have been very successful in the past. I would like to think I could be successful in the future.'

He conceded he was 'slightly unorthodox' in the way he conducted his business and was reluctant to keep up with paperwork and emails.

'I arrange the deals, then I hand them over to highly paid professionals like yourselves' – lawyers – 'to do the business,' he told Mr Howling.

He described his former solicitor Stanley Beller as 'my worst enemy'.

'I find it difficult saying his first name,' said Young.

Mr Howling put it to the tycoon that: 'You deliberately distanced yourself from your assets and tried to put your assets beyond her [Mrs Young's] reach.'

Young denied this, saying the barrister had 'got it horribly wrong again'.

When Mr Howling asked him if he felt uneasy, Young replied: 'I'm totally relaxed.'

Young was asked about an affidavit sworn by Kevin Cash in 2007 saying that he had benefited from a variety of lucrative ventures with several well-known businessmen. Young replied that he was only involved in one project with any of the men – a £100-million venture called 'EU Smart' with Sir Philip Green and Sir Tom Hunter. He also admitted discussing business dealings with Boris Berezovsky, including the possibility of Young helping the late Russian oligarch to fund one of the Ukrainian presidential hopefuls.

The court was told that the tycoon hid out in Germany for eighteen months after he claimed to have lost all his money in 2006. Mr Howling asked him if he was in Germany setting up a branch of Soho House with Richard Caring. Young said: 'I had absolutely nothing to do with this.'

The High Court heard companies and entities owned by Jonathan Brown, a smoked salmon businessman who Mr Young claimed he owed £3.3 million, had recently sent money to him through third parties. Stephen Kay, another person who had paid into Project Moscow, also provided him with support.

'Jonathan Brown and Stephen Kay are in litigation with you yet they are still providing you with financial support,' said Mr Howling

'These guys... I begged them to help the family,' Young replied.

Asking about Young's financial arrangements with Jonathan

Brown, Mr Howling said: "Why would he feel the need to continue to help you? You are in litigation with him in Miami, in France. He would have every reason to be fed up with you, wouldn't he, because he is supposed to be a debtor to Project Moscow? Why would he remain friends with you if you owe him £3.3 million?"

'Mr Brown was initially very unhappy with me,' said Young. 'But now we are close friends.'

Mr Howling found this hard to believe.

'The whole debt is a fabrication, isn't it Mr Young,' he said. 'This is all part of a sham."

'Absolutely not,' said Young faultingly. 'He's obviously... he's obviously... he's a very good friend.'

The court later heard that all the debts to investors in Project Moscow had been paid off, including more than £4 million that had gone to the daughter of Boris Berezovsky. This was curious as Project Moscow had been given as the very reason that Scot Young was broke.

When Howling asked further questions about Project Moscow, Young told him to speak to Stephen Jones, the lawyer who had constructed the deal, who was due to give evidence the following week. Jones had already made an application to exclude the press from the proceedings when he testified to protect the confidentiality of his clients.

There was more. The questioning moved on to a major £200 million property development in central London. 'Project Mayfair' at 56 Curzon Street was recorded as an asset of the bankrupt tycoon in a 2006 schedule of his holdings held by Fox Williams. Emails concerning it recovered from the laptop Young had given to his daughters were read out. One suggested that Mr Young was looking to buy £40 million of shares in a Jersey-based company through a firm called Fortdale Properties Ltd, which was ultimately under the control of the 'International Family Fund'. This was another venture mentioned in other emails.

'It's beginning to look like, Mr Young, that you were intending to buy the shares in Arden Ltd through the use of Fortdale Properties Ltd,' said Mr Justice Moor.

Young denied this and denied owning any interest in Project Mayfair. But Mr Justice Moor was unmoved.

'There is a link in relation to Curzon Street,' he said. 'I will have to make a finding of fact about it.'

Young was then accused of defrauding the Bank of Scotland when he had lied to Fox Williams, telling them that he owned three million shares in the telecoms giant O_2 in order to secure a loan from HBOS to buy his house in Miami.

In tense exchanges with the judge, Mr Young refused four times to admit he had lied about owning £6-million of shares.

'If you didn't own these shares then you are defrauding the Bank of Scotland,' Mr Howling said. 'If it's not fraud, what is it?'

But Young refused to be drawn. He asked the judge to put questions about the matter to his former lawyer Paul Osborne, who was due to give evidence the following week.

Next he was questioned about his involvement with a company called BTG Europe. The attendance notes of two lawyers' meetings were read out in court. In them, Young is described as the 'beneficial owner' and a 'shareholder'. Again, Young denied having any interest in the company. Mr Howling did not believe him.

'Why else would you be recorded as being part of that empire?" he asked.

Mr Justice Moor was also sceptical.

'I'm not quite sure why you'd be there at all if you weren't involved,' he said.

'I am not lying' was Young's facile rebuttal.

The court also heard there was more than £150 million 'flushing' through some of Mr Young's bank accounts that remained unaccounted for.

'I totally resent that,' Young replied. 'You can't make money disappear, my Lord.'

Plainly this was not true. Mr Howling noted that a forensic analysis of Mr Young's bank accounts showed a phenomenal amount of money had simply vanished into thin air.

'There was £134 million of cash movement through your various accounts between January 2004 and October 2009,' he said. 'A total of £80 million of payments were made to Mr Young, for which no entries were found in the bank statements provided.'

Young then said he could not recall why he had invested 1 million euros in a Finnish-based company called Liekki Oy, which held lucrative patents in laser technology. Not only that. He denied holding an interest in the company and said it was linked to Mr Kay. However, Mr Howling read out other emails and attendance notes that showed Young had 'command and control' of the company, while Kay was nowhere to be seen.

'On the face of it, Mr Young, it is inconsistent, isn't it?' said Mr Justice Moor. 'Mr Kay should have been doing this.'

All Young could do was repeat his denial in relation to Liekki Oy.

Then Young was questioned about the Post-it note seized in 2012 that mentioned the Facebook flotation and a share deal involving the social network's first president, Silicon Valley giant Sean Parker. On it, Mr Young had written: 'Will make $4.5 billion.'

'This is just a random piece of paper with my scribbling,' Young insisted. 'Can I state for the record I have never owned shares in Facebook in any shape or form?'

PROJECT MARRIAGE WALK

Mr Howling asked why Young had paid out a £200,000 deposit on two villas in February 2006, during the period of his supposed financial meltdown.

'If you knew you were already in difficulty,' asked the QC, 'why were you investing £200,000 in that sort of project?'

Young justified the investment on the grounds that he 'was getting it at a very good discount'.

And why he had received emails and service charges bills for London properties he claimed not to own?

'I think it's a little bit unfair that I'm being asked to prove a negative,' Young said.

He was also questioned on a labyrinth of companies that he allegedly used to hide his vast fortune.

Mr Young insisted that these were all public companies. But Mr Howling said that did not prevent the tycoon from owning small or large shareholdings, something Young should have disclosed to the court.

He was questioned about 'smurfing', which is technically the practice of breaking down a transaction into smaller transactions that leave no record. It is used in money laundering. For example, under the Money Laundering Regulations of 2003, a bank is obliged to report any cash transaction worth over 15,000 euros. Mr Young was, apparently, unfamiliar with the term.

'I'm not a smurf,' he said. 'I don't know what a smurf is.'

Young was then asked about a meeting he had had with his wife in August 2009, where she asked for £1 billion and he made a counter-offer of £300 million. This was, he said, 'a complete and utter joke'. He had been drinking the night before and was ashamed of what he said.

Details of the offer in August 2009 emerged in an 'opening note' that Young had written. Mr Justice Moor said journalists could see the note, although Mr Young said he would 'rather they didn't'. After outlining the offer, the note went on: '[I am] ashamed to say, [I] stated that if Ronald Regan [sic] became the next US president [he was already dead], Jeremy Beadle [of the TV programme *You've Been Framed*], walked through the door and the Tooth Fairy arrived, she could have the money.'

Young apologised to the court for being so flippant, but he said the 'suggestion was so ridiculous that I thought I would make it even more ridiculous'.

When questioned about the note, Young told the judge: 'I was all over the place. I had been drinking heavily the night before. My wife asked for a billion. I was trying to say how ridiculous the situation was. I had no money and that was it.'

Mr Howling said: 'You don't make comments like that unless you've got the money.'

When the lawyer Stephen Jones of consultants Jirehouse Capital was called to give evidence, he again asked the judge to bar reporters from the courtroom during his cross-examination to protect the confidentiality of his clients. However, Mr Justice Moor refused to order journalists to leave the court after reporters argued that Mr Jones should be treated in the same way as other witnesses. The judge said he would hear Mr Jones's evidence then decide whether journalists should be prevented from reporting any aspect of it.

At it was, Jones frequently avoided answering questions by citing legal privilege. However, he did deny helping Mr Young create a 'sham' bankruptcy. In the end, Mr Justice Moor ruled that all of Mr Jones's evidence could be reported and a barrister representing Mr Jones raised no objection.

Veteran forensic accountant Carl Biggs was then called. He had examined financial papers that Mr Young had released in response to court orders. Biggs told the court: 'I don't see how Mr Young could have possibly become a bankrupt with the figures I have seen. I think the most important thing is I did not get full disclosure of all the accounts. Mr Young made income or gains in excess of £40 million in a seven-year period, and he lost £3 million. I cannot see how Mr Young could have possibly become a bankrupt based on the figures I have seen. It is as simple as that. Where's the money gone? I haven't seen where it's gone.'

He also said he could not understand how Bank of Scotland and others were listed as creditors on the 'business affidavit' Young submitted to the court. Biggs said: 'Having read his affidavit, I have been unable to locate any other borrowings to justify these creditors.'

Other experts were equally baffled. Mark Bezant, senior managing director of FTI Consulting, told the High Court that he and his team spent five months trying produce a chart outlining the structure of Young's business empire and 'an overlapping of activity' between the property mogul and his associates. The resulting diagram was too large to be displayed in court. It was, he said, the size of a dinner table. Even so, they had identified 'a large number of gaps in the information set.... In short, it appears that Mr Young's disclosure was incomplete and, in some respects, disingenuous,' he said. 'We had identified areas where we considered his disclosure to be incomplete, inconsistent or incorrect in some way and we then developed that into this report.'

Bezant lamented how little co-operation Mr Young had given, despite court orders and admitted FTI Consulting were 'unable to trace the source and destination' of some of the funds. The next stage of the investigation, he said, should target a further eight management companies, thirty banks and thirty law firms who all had ties to Young.

Mr Howling said the chart appeared 'to display a spider's web of interconnections' between shell companies. Mr Justice Moor said he tried to look at the chart, but 'it looked very complicated', while Young said: 'It's gobbledegook to me.'

Bezant said 'deficiencies' in Young's disclosure included the O_2 shares, the proceeds from the sale of Dione, IAC Holdings, Acme, Tictocology, Allied Minds, BTG and Gold Oil. Young said he was struggling to understand the evidence due to 'an altercation with the paparazzi' that morning.

Poju Zabludowicz was called. He admitted funding two ventures with Young – a chip-and-pin technology company called Dione and the Russian property deal known as Project Moscow. But he denied holding any interest in a company called BTG.

Mr Howling asked Mr Zabludowicz about a BTG attendance note, dated September 2005 and recovered from Young's laptop, that said 'SY and PZ' were 'funders/beneficial owners' of BTG. One of the men recorded as being present at the meeting was David Halpern, one of Zabludowicz's financial advisers.

'I was not,' said the billionaire. 'Perhaps one of my trusts was, but I was not.'

Asked if Young was a funder or beneficial owner of BTG, Zabludowicz said: 'I don't know.'

He was also read a letter from Young's former lawyer, Stanley Beller, addressed to the 'Zabludowicz Trust' and dated a few months earlier. It said: 'We are delighted to know that you and Mr Young are going to complete the purchase of a hundred per cent share capital of BTG.'

Mr Howling asked: 'Was Mr Beller writing to that trust because you were intending to buy the shares?'

Zabludowicz replied: 'I don't recall.'

He did admit being involved in Project Moscow, but when

asked how much money he had put in, he said: 'I can't remember the exact interest.'

The billionaire was similarly uninformative when he was asked what he knew about an email recovered from Mr Young's wiped hard drive that read: 'SY no longer has a requirement for tax-planning as he can already use off-shore SPVs [Special Purpose Vehicles] set up by Poju Zabludowicz.'

He said simply: 'I don't know.'

Next the court heard from James Creed, who said he had been friends with Mr Young for twenty years. Despite being a bankrupt, he admitted borrowing £50,000 against his own home to lend Young money to pay his legal fees.

'Why would you expose yourself to future financial risk by borrowing money to assist Scot Young?' asked Mr Howling.

'He is my friend and he needed help,' Mr Creed replied.

Mr Howling then pointed out that account ledgers from one of Young's former lawyers showed the bankrupt Mr Creed had lent Young £600,000 over the years.

'I have never had £600,000,' Creed said.

Despite his earlier protests, Sir Philip Green did turn up in court. In a statement, he said: 'Scot explained his financial position to me and explained the problems he was having. He asked me if I could help, which I agreed to do. I made two payments to an estate agent of £50,000 and £30,000 – I believe to pay some rent. I was providing the money to Scot Young, who paid it to his other half, Mrs Young, as a favour... This came from my personal bank account.'

He told the judge: 'I have known Mr Young for about ten or fifteen years. I got introduced to him. I cannot remember how or where. I sort of became a friend. I wasn't in business with him. I believe my family was offered an investment, among many other people, and I think we made an investment in that company.'

During that time, he had met Mrs Young only once.

He was then asked: 'What was your impression of Mr Young's wealth, prior to his "demise" as he puts it, in March 2006? Was he a man of substance?'

Green replied: 'No idea. I assume he was doing business. He was comfortable. I don't ask people I do business with what their banks statements are.'

Mr Howling said Mrs Young's case was that Scot Young 'continues to have a considerable amount of money and members of his social circle have helped him secrete this money away from the courts'. Asked whether he had had any involvement in such a process, Green answered: 'Zero.'

Did he help Young 'secrete' money or assets?

Green replied tersely: 'No.'

Asked about the £80,000 he had given Scot Young, Green said that £50,000 was for the 'purpose of providing part of the deposit' for the purchase of a property in September 2008 and a further £30,000 for the 'purpose of rent' in December 2008

Was it to support Mrs Young and the couple's two children? Green said: 'I provided the money to Mr Young. That happened to be on behalf of Mrs Young as a favour. Clearly, I haven't got it back.' But he said he thought that, if Young got back into business, the loan would be repaid.

Green was asked whether he stood by his statement that the cash was a loan, not a gift. He replied: 'I don't suppose I would swear a statement that was untrue.'

As he walked out of the courtroom after giving evidence, Green threw a cheque on to the desk of Mrs Young's barrister and said: 'Give this back to your client.' Apparently the cheque, which was for £50, had been sent to Sir Philip to cover his travelling expenses.

The court also heard from Richard Caring, who admitted that

he lent Young £50,000 in 2009 because he was his friend and he wanted to help. In a statement, he said: 'The reason I lent Mr Young this money is that I have know him for many years and he explained his financial position to me and explained the problems he was having. I decided to help him and his family.'

He had known Young for over twenty years.

'I said I would lend him the money on the basis that if there was a time that he could repay it, that would be great, if there wasn't, there wasn't,' he said. 'I don't really expect Scot to repay me the money. The least I could do was try and help him in some way.'

Caring denied that he and his circle had cut off the finance after deciding Mrs Young was 'trying to embarrass them in the press'.

Ruslan Formichev also said he had lent Young £10,000 in 2006, but said he had not repaid it, despite repeated reminders.

Michael Slater gave evidence on behalf of Kevin Cash. Asked about the money, he said: 'If Scot Young borrowed money, he borrowed money from my client.'

Shown a document listing Mr Young's assets, Slater remarked that it was 'a wonderful work of fiction'.

'How would you know that if you don't represent Mr Young?' Mr Howling asked.

'I noticed an asset – number 13,' said Slater. 'It's a property belonging to my client. It's down there being worth £13 million – it's worth £2 million.'

He was also asked about ledger accounts from Mr Young's corporate lawyers that showed his own firm, Butcher Burns, was paid £7.25 million.

'I have no idea,' said Slater.

However, he admitted handing Young £5,000 in cash on behalf of a client.

The High Court also heard from Willie Raeburn of Lloyds Banking Group. Mr Raeburn confirmed that one of his colleagues, Alastair Kennedy, had seen millions of pounds in share certificates belonging to Mr Young when he visited the office of Young's former lawyer, Stanley Beller, in 2006.

The assets held by the lawyer had been used to guarantee a bridging loan to the tycoon on a £6 million beachfront property in Miami.

Mr Raeburn said: 'Mr Kennedy told me that he had seen the share certificates.'

Meanwhile in a separate case in the High Court involving his former lawyer and an alleged creditor, Young was denounced as a fraudster. Elizabeth Sears claimed she was owed £100,000 by Stanley Beller. In a judgment handed down in the court of costs, Master Colin Campbell found the money had been paid back to Ms Sears in 2007 by Mr Young via Stephen Jones, though he claimed he has never acted for the bankrupt businessman.

In reaching his findings, the judge relied on emails between Young and Jones in his role at Jirehouse.

'The first states that Mr Jones was not sure "if Stanley was even involved in the matter" being a reference to "the loan Liz [Sears] made to you",' said Master Campbell. 'The second says: "And by the way, thank you for all the many happy times I have spent at your house in Miami conjuring up plans to screw Beller."'

Master Campbell concluded: 'The correspondence that Jirehouse's solicitors, in conjunction with Mr Young, were "conjuring up plans to screw Beller", speaks for itself.'

Master Campbell labelled the tycoon the 'fraudster Scot Young' in reference to a previous case, presided over by Lord Justice Thomas. In 2009, that judge found that Young had defrauded Mr Beller. As a result the lawyer could 'no longer comply with undertakings he had made on behalf of his client'. He was then struck off by the Solicitors Regulation Authority.

Lord Justice Thomas said of Beller in 2009: 'It is no defence to say that he was duped; he was plainly duped, but... being duped by your own client is no excuse.'

There was more bad news for Scot Young in the Sears case. A forensic accountant told the court that Young wrote a £6 million cheque to his creditor, Ms Sears, just before he claims to have lost all his money.

Once again Stephen Jones claimed his firm had nothing to do with Scot Young. He told the *Independent on Sunday*: 'We have never acted for Scot Young and merely facilitated a settlement with his creditors. The matter of any cheque paid to Ms Sears is a matter you should address with her. It has nothing to do with us.'

CHAPTER 16

LEGAL HISTORY

Back in the family court, Mr Justice Moor told Michelle Young that she might have missed an opportunity when she rejected a £300 million offer from Mr Young four years earlier – 'if it was genuine'.

'Why didn't she accept it?' he asked. 'Gift horse and mouth come to mind.'

In what had come to be one of the longest divorce cases in British legal history, Mr Howling told Mr Justice Moor that Mrs Young had run up a bill of £1.6 million before beginning his concluding remarks.

'This is one of those cases... which is like trying to locate a submarine without sonar,' he told the judge. 'We have had periscope sightings during the course of these proceedings.'

Indicating Mr Young, he said: 'He was and continues to be a man who has access to considerable sums of money. And not just the odd million or two... What we see sight of is inconsistent with a penniless bankrupt.'

The judge agreed.

'His lifestyle is not consistent with being a penniless bankrupt. He has wads of cash in his possession,' he said.

Young continued to describe this as 'nonsense'.

Giving his ruling, Mr Justice Moor said: 'This case has been quite extraordinary even by the standards of the most bitter matrimonial breakdowns. Extremely serious allegations have been bandied around like confetti. The case has cost the wife millions of pounds. It has taken six-and-a-half years to come to trial. There have been sixty-five hearings.'

Both were to blame.

'I have to be highly critical of the way in which the case has been conducted at various times by both parties. In many respects, this is about as bad an example of how not to litigate as any I have ever encountered,' the judgment read. 'I feel nothing but sympathy for the two children of these parties. Through no fault of their own, their parents' marriage broke down.

'A marital breakdown is distressing enough for any child, but for the divorce to then be played out in the full glare of the media must have been absolutely appalling for them. What has occurred has not been child focused. I truly hope that the parents will reflect on this.'

But he was not entirely unsympathetic to the contenders.

'It is a sad fact that both parties have suffered from serious ill-health during the course of these proceedings,' he said. 'I have made orders preventing the media from reporting any details in relation to the husband and I would have made a similar order in relation to the wife had I been asked. There is, however, no restriction against reporting what now follows.'

He went on: 'I do not intend to deal further with health issues other than to say three things. First, there have been suggestions by the wife at times that the husband was feigning his ill-health. I reject that completely. I have seen the medical reports and I accept them.

'Second, I do accept that the strain of this litigation is likely to have been a contributing factor to the ill-health of both these parties. Third, I do not consider it necessary to go into further detail because it does not appear to me that their health is relevant to the exercise I have to perform.

'So far as the wife is concerned, I very much hope that her ill-health is completely behind her. So far as the husband is concerned, he has not said that he is unable to work going forward. Provided he takes his medication and absent the strain of these proceedings, I am satisfied that he will be able to control his health difficulties and rebuild his life.'

The couple's fortunes had reflected the UK's property and technology booms and busts. They started with virtually nothing, the judge observed. 'Their standard of living increased exponentially... The husband says the family lived beyond its means but he was not, in any way, a reluctant spender.'

Again he reprimanded Mrs Young for not accepting £300 million when it was offered.

'I do not question in any way her honesty,' said the judge. 'I regret to say, however, that I do not consider her evidence to be reliable. She has become utterly convinced that her husband is a liar who has hidden vast resources. She sees conspiracy everywhere. She is convinced that the husband engineered his financial meltdown in the early part of 2006 knowing that his marriage was to end. She believes this was with the sole purpose of keeping his assets safe from her claims. She is convinced that, if the husband once owned a property, he must still own it today.'

Responding to the judge's chiding later, Michelle insisted that everything she had unearthed was true.

'I know it must be difficult for people to follow,' she said. 'It's like a movie.'

As for Mrs Young's ambition to live in a 'prime central London location', Mr Justice Moor said: 'If the husband is worth hundreds of millions of pounds, as she contends, it would be perfectly reasonable for her to own a £20 million property in Belgravia but, if he is not, she will have to set her sights somewhat lower.'

Mr Young also came in for a reprimand from the judge. He had 'failed to give full and frank disclosure' about his assets and 'is hiding the truth'.

'There remains a cloak hiding the true financial position of the husband,' said Mr Justice Moor and he could only accept his evidence if it was corroborated from another source.

'Mr Young has misled the court very significantly as to his financial position,' said the judge. 'Effectively, he has been responsible for this litigation. It is undoubtedly the most difficult financial remedy case I have ever come across...'

The problem was that the judge could still not make up his mind what Scot Young was worth.

'It is completely impossible to produce any sort of schedule of the husband's assets in 2006 due to the significant number of lies told by the husband to so many people over such a long period. Doing as best I can, I find that he still has £45 million hidden from this court. As against that, I must deduct £5 million for his debts, making a net total of £40 million. The wife is entitled to half, namely a lump sum of £20 million.'

That seemed fair.

'I only have two things to say,' said the judge. 'First, this debt will exist for all time. The husband will never be free of it. It is in his interests to discharge it so he can move on. Second, I have rejected all the more fanciful allegations made against him. I cannot see how he would have complied with an order for a lump sum of £300 million, let alone £400 million. I hope he will take the view he is better off paying the £20 million so that he can concentrate on rebuilding his life.'

Mrs Young was outraged. Only £20 million!

'It's disgraceful. I stand by what I said. He's worth billions,' she told a gaggle of reporters outside the court. 'This has been a desperate struggle for me and my two daughters, cast adrift seven years ago by a powerful maniac who felt he could hide his vast wealth behind his super-rich friends, blue-chip institution and the law-enforcement agencies who would rather turn the other cheek than tackle corruption. My husband has been allowed to make a mockery of the justice system for seven years, lying and cheating at every turn... He has repeatedly failed to disclose how he lost his money, which has led Mr Justice Moor to draw the inevitable conclusion: he has hidden a fortune...'

She was now on her high horse.

'...This case has uncovered some dark truths about the Britain we all live in today. This city is too reliant on industrial-scale fraud and money laundering, aided by corrupt bankers and accountants. Many people will think it's a fortune but at the moment, all this order is, is a piece of paper. I will need to borrow heavily against this award to fund an asset recovery mission, the like of which I doubt this country will have seen. So this isn't over. Not for me, not for my two daughters, and not for Mr Young.'

She was wrong. Mr Justice Moor refused permission to appeal against his judgement.

Mrs Young's lawyer Catherine Thomas said: 'This case has been among the most complex in English divorce law history, in which a number of high-profile witnesses were called. Michelle's legal team believes our detailed approach to assessing Mr Young's true wealth has been instrumental in securing this substantial payout for Michelle and her children. The verdict sends a strong message to those across the world seeking to hide their true wealth from their spouse – even the most intricate of financial arrangements can be exposed by specialist law firms.'

The kindly judge then returned Mr Young's passport to him. This allowed Scot and Noelle to take a holiday in Bali – paid for by one of his wealthy friends, of course. It was their first foreign trip together. Noelle was unrepentant about taking another hand-out.

'He's made a lot of money for a lot of people over the years,' she said.

When Young was asked about his wife's reaction to the ruling, he said: 'Disgraceful? That was my wife's quote was it? No comment.'

Michelle later pointed out that, when she said disgraceful: 'I in no way meant the ruling of the judge, but rather the way in which Scot has skilfully hidden our assets, declared himself bankrupt and still not complied with court orders. I am very pleased that the British legal system has acknowledged he has a multi-million pound fortune with which he should have supported his daughters.'

Mr Young was also ordered to pay £5 million towards his ex-wife's legal costs. In his written judgement, Mr Justice Moor said: 'In one sense, the wife did amazingly well to be able to obtain as much litigation funding as she did, given that she had no security to offer. The amounts spent, however, are truly eye-watering.'

The husband should pay up because the legal fees were built up due to his refusal to provide 'full disclosure' of his financial circumstances. Young was also £1.6 million in arrears with maintenance.

'I can see no reason why the husband should not pay the lump sum quickly, given that half the money he had in 2006 was held in shares which would have been readily realisable,' Mr Justice Moor said.

However, he conceded that Mrs Young might never see any money out of the case.

'I realise Mrs Young will have difficulty enforcing this order,' the judge said. 'The husband has not complied with court orders. He has... not made any reasonable offer to settle the proceedings. He has been found to have misled the court as to his finances to a very significant extent. On the other hand, the wife has raised issues that I have found to be completely unfounded.'

However, the judge had come to the conclusion that Mr Young was 'not a penniless man of straw with huge debts' and that the 'wads of cash' being handed to the tycoon by his friends 'came from his own hidden resources, in part held for him by third parties'. He concluded that almost all of the debts that led Mr Young to be declared bankrupt in 2010 did not now exist. He also said that Mr Young had stolen £20 million in share certificates from his former lawyer Stanley Beller in 2006, and had also received other payments totalling another £20 million, which he had never revealed to the court. He found that Mr Young still owned properties held in other people's names. But the judge had no idea what had happened to his fortune.

None of Mrs Young's allegations against Simon Cowell, Sir Philip Green and Richard Caring could be substantiated, the judge said. He 'entirely and unreservedly' accepted the evidence given to the court by Sir Philip and Mr Caring about their loans to Mr Young. The judge also cleared Paul Osborne from the corporate law firm Fox Williams and Stephen Jones of Jirehouse Capital of any wrongdoing. Nevertheless, something had gone awry.

'Overall, there is no doubt that the husband has not given full and frank disclosure,' said the judge. 'The central question as to how he lost his money remains unanswered.'

Unbowed by the paltry settlement, Mrs Young continued in full campaigning mode.

'My case has exposed the woeful shortcomings of the family law system,' she said. 'I have made a stand for women. I don't want to go through all this for nothing, I want to see the law changed to protect women like me with children by men who conveniently find they suddenly have no assets when they want to go off with a younger woman. I think and hope this case is making history.

'One woman told me she had been in this process for eight years, and it needs a strong woman to stand up to the system. I am fighting as a woman and a mother and with dignity. I am proud to stand up to him. I think and hope this case is making history.'

Again, Danae Brook at the *Daily Telegraph* was right behind her.

'When she met Scot Young in 1988 he was an ambitious young entrepreneur yet to make millions in property and technology, while she worked in retail. The couple had so little money that they lived with Mrs Young's parents before they married in 1995,' she wrote.

Then in the eleven-year marriage there were the mansions, the yacht, the £1million wedding rings and haute-cuisine meals at £5,000 a time. Cut to November 2006. She was getting dressed in their £6 million Miami beach house when the fateful phone call came telling her that he had lost it all. She did not believe it for a moment, but she did not realise what a fight she had on her hands.

Meanwhile Michelle and the girls moved into a two-bedroom flat paid for partly out of housing benefit. Nevertheless, it was in a smart, though discreet building with a doorman and an impressive lobby.

'We have had to move four times in five years – all our personal belongings including books, clothes, pictures, are in storage,' Michelle said. 'We are living from hand to mouth. I share a room with my younger daughter, I don't take them anywhere, I don't even know where or how they get their clothes and I don't go shopping at all any more... It's been absolutely devastating for the girls. We have downscaled by a huge amount in our lifestyles, but that hasn't really bothered me so much because I am one of those people, I just face whatever comes along.'

She has no car and says she has not had a holiday in three years. With no cleaner, she and the girls do their own chores and her younger daughter had to complete her education in a state school. They both went on to university in London – Scarlet read English literature and Sasha studied business – and continued to live with their mother.

'But that's fine – that's just normal, isn't it?' she said. 'My girls aren't princesses – they never have been. I've raised them to always tidy up by themselves.'

Pursuing the case, she woke at five or six every morning to go through the legal papers. There were 128,000 digital and 40,000 hard copy documents to go through in all. But by 8 am she was on her exercise bike, though regularly broke off from her routine to take calls from one of her many lawyers.

'I have been working twelve to fourteen hours a day,' she

said. 'I know almost by heart every tiny piece of the case, every letter, figure, statement. Emotionally and physically it's been draining.'

Asked about what she was living on, she told the *MailOnline*: 'I'd rather not talk to you about that but all I can say is that I've had help from friends, family and unsecured loans, which I have had to use. I have had so many sleepless nights worrying that we are going to have to move again. That is something many women will understand – it's just one part of the big battle you have when you are dealing with someone who is refusing to be fair at the end of a marriage.'

And she was dedicated to the cause.

'I've had to learn about forensic accounting, law, how assets are concealed off-shore – and I've done all that by reading the files myself and putting the proposals together,' she said. Although she was a stay-at-home wife and mother during her seventeen years with Young, she pointed out that she 'never lost [her] business acumen'.

On her days in court, her eyes were red from exhaustion. Unable to afford fine food, she was unhealthily skinny and her lank hair had not been cut for months. Standards had begun to slip. She complained that she had 'no time to prepare or think about what I was going to wear'. She still displayed the trappings of her previous life – Hermès handbags and Vivienne Westwood suits.

By contrast, Noelle Reno's hair was lustrous, her skin glowing and her outfit up-to-date – though Scot Young himself cultivated a shabby look.

Referring to her ex-husband impersonally as 'Scot Young', Michelle said: 'To me, he looks emotionless, with no feelings. There should be some guilt, some shame, some remorse for what he has done, if not to me then to our children. If you loved your children you wouldn't do this sort of thing to them, no matter what he says about loving them. When I see him it makes my skin crawl.'

With all the work she had put in on the case, she had had no time for leisure activities and certainly no time for a new relationship.

'I don't even have time to think about missing having a man, a husband, a lover,' she said. 'But it is obviously something which will come back into my life and I look forward to that. I am sure it will happen once this is resolved.'

Could she ever trust a man again?

'Some of my best friends are men,' she said.

Would Scarlet and Sasha be scarred by seeing what she had gone through with their father?

'There is a difference between one man and men in general,' said Michelle. 'I have talked with them about that and they understand. So I know they will be fine.'

Meanwhile she doubts that her ex-husband will pay up – after having failed to comply with court orders for seven years.

'Mr Young has clearly played a numbers game,' she said. 'He looked at the strategy and decided he would keep more money through non-disclosure and playing the system, rather than award me and my girls the settlement we deserve. Sadly for us, and for Mr Justice Moor, it has been impossible to quantify the assets that he has hidden, which has resulted in this reduced award.'

CHAPTER 17

THE LAST MOVE

The judgement was made in November 2013. On 14 March 2014, Michelle was back in court, complaining that she had not received a penny of the £26 million settlement that had been awarded to her.

'I do feel there is a real air of unreality in this case,' Mr Justice Moor told Mrs Young's counsel James Bogle. 'On my finding on the evidence Mr Young has hidden his assets off-shore. Your client has spent £7 million and not been able to find anything. Nobody has been able to find any money at all.'

As Scot Young was still officially bankrupt, all Scot Young's assets were technically owned by his trustee-in-bankruptcy, David Ingram of Grant Thornton. So Mrs Young took action against them. As she had failed in a bid to force Grant Thornton to hold a public meeting to explain why they had not been able to recover any funds, she made an application to have the firm replaced by a new firm of trustees. By then,

Grant Thornton had spent £900,000 searching for Mr Young's assets over and above the money she had spent on the task. But the judge decided that the case was now a matter for the bankruptcy courts, where Mr Young's case would resume later in that year. Mrs Young was ordered to pay the costs of the failed application.

The judge added: 'It is not clear to me why anyone wants to be in charge of this case when no-one has recovered any money at all.'

He then formally transferred the case to the bankruptcy court where a fresh hearing was scheduled for May. As the judge had already refused her permission to appeal against his ruling, she had no choice but to abandon any further action against her ex-husband in the family courts. But still Michelle was undaunted.

'What he never thought would happen was that I would get a judgment order that has made me the largest creditor in his bankruptcy,' she said.

However, this meant she had to assemble a new legal team of insolvency, rather than divorce, specialists, who had agreed to work on a recovery – or no win, no fee – basis.

'In the family courts, it has been difficult to get behind the bankruptcy issue,' she said. 'Quite often husbands use bankruptcy as a vehicle to stop proceedings. But I now have the best legal brains in the country working to bring this case to a conclusion through the insolvency courts.'

What amazed those who met her was that she still had the stamina to carry on. Though she was happy to pose for photographers, showing off her slim, sylphlike figure, her face was growing lined with care and the newspapers commented on the permanent frown across her forehead.

'There are days when I feel my energy has been drained, but

I always find this inner strength,' she told *MailOnline*. 'People approach me and say, "Michelle, we know you are a fighter," and I think that comes from my background and from what we have been through over the past eight years.'

She got her strength from her father, who died in 2009, she said. He was 'my rock – he brought me up to believe nothing was impossible'.

What's more, despite all she had gone through, she was optimistic.

'I'm in a good place because the end is in sight,' she said. And she believed that she would get the money owing to her. What would she do with it?

'I don't think about that because this is not about the amount of money, it is about what is morally correct,' she said. 'But it will give me and the girls the security that we have been deprived of for the past eight years.'

She also expressed her ambition to establish a foundation that would help other divorcees. It was to be called the Michelle Young Foundation and would campaign for tougher laws surrounding non-disclosure in divorce cases. In Californian law 'would-be hiders' face jail terms of up to four years and much harsher fines. It would also support others fighting for a fair share of their spouse's assets.

'It is not just me going through this,' she said. 'This is happening every day in courts across the country. Non-disclosure is fraud and fraud is theft. And what keeps me striving forward is my two girls and all the other families who have been wronged. People who hide their assets are also hiding from the taxman, so disclosure is in everyone's interest.'

Michelle had poured her own money – and other people's – into the cause. More than £4 million had come from litigation funding. First there was £400,000 from Harbour. Another

£1 million came from Bracewell Law. Then she reached an agreement with a company called ASCL and others for £2.7 million. The rest came from three separate law firms on the promise of a sizeable cut in her eventual settlement. She believed that their confidence validated 'the strengths and merits of the case'. It certainly spoke volumes for her tenacity.

There was not just lawyers to pay: forensic accountants FTI Consulting were paid £500,000 for their investigation and there was a claim against her for another £300,000. Two other firms of investigators, Alvarez and Marsal and Guidepost Solutions, then had to start again from scratch, claiming £800,000 and £700,000 respectively.

By that time Michelle had been through thirteen sets of lawyers and four teams of forensic accountants.

'She has a habit of falling out with people,' said one of them.

Worse was to come. She was duped into paying £14,000 to a man claiming to be a former MI6 agent who said he could trace her husband's money for her.

In July 2014, she was approached by Mark Hill-Wood, who told her he had worked for twenty-five years for GCHQ and the Secret Intelligence Service before setting up his own private detective agency, Full-Proof Intelligence, which operated out of a postal box in the City.

His LinkedIn page described him as a 'highly respected operative who formerly worked in the Intelligence Services' and he specialised in cyber investigations, firearms training and 'suspect interrogation'.

According to the *Independent on Sunday*, Mr Hill-Wood told Ms Young that he had come across some of her former husband's hidden wealth in a Swiss bank account while working on an assignment in Russia. She raised his fee from her litigation funders.

Hill-Wood said he would travel to Russia himself to recover the documentary evidence. However, suspicions were raised when an email came from what purported to be another employee of FullProof Intelligence saying Hill-Wood had been captured by the Russians who were going to hold him until another £15,000 was raised. Ms Young refused to send the money and Hill-Wood eventually emailed to say he had been released.

By the end of July, Hill-Wood claimed he had returned to the UK with 'two lever-arch files' of material that supposedly detailed Mr Young's off-shore wealth. However he repeatedly cancelled meetings with her and her QC where he was supposed to hand it over. At one point, Mrs Young emailed, begging him to hand it over, saying: 'I feel like crying, I'm under so much pressure.' But the files never materialised and Mrs Young reported him to the police.

It turned out that, rather than being a spook, Hill-Wood was an inveterate con-man. He had a prolific career in deception under the name Phillip Buffett and had previously been dubbed the 'fantasy fraudster' by a judge.

In 2012, he had been given a two-year suspended sentence for conning Harrods out of luxury goods worth over £245,000. Buffett used dud cheques to pay for a £216,000 Hublot watch, a second one costing £20,000, clothes, a camera and other luxury items.

When he appeared in court, he was wearing a red Ralph Lauren polo shirt. The judge asked: 'Why the Ralph Lauren clothing? I'm assuming it's not the real brand.'

Buffett protested it was genuine. The judge replied: 'Well, I'm glad you can afford it. What's wrong with M&S?'

The judge also questioned his choice of accessories.

'How you ever thought you could buy a watch worth £216,000

absolutely stuns me. Why anyone would want a watch worth £216,000 also stuns me. I don't wear a watch, and haven't for thirty or forty years. I don't need one.'

Based in Croydon, South London, Buffett had served time for previous offences of fraud. Using the name Mark Castley he had duped elite British athletes with the promise of lucrative sponsorship contracts in exchange for 'membership fees' of up to £1,000 in the run-up to the 2012 London Olympics.

Buffett used Harrods' 'By Appointment' shopper service to pull off his latest scam, paying with cheques from an account that had been closed. He pawned the Hublot watch and took £77,000 to go to the Monaco Grand Prix, where he was photographed alongside commentator and former racing driver David Coulthard. While there, Buffett tried to obtain a 'luxury package' to watch the Monaco Grand Prix, including hospitality on the Mercedes F1 yacht. He was arrested at Gatwick Airport on his return.

The forty-nine-year-old admitted seven counts of fraud against businesses and individuals, totalling another £119,000, as well as breaching a ban on him acting as a company director. These offences were committed through a number of firms he set up under the umbrella of Über Intelligence – in breach of a seven-year company directorship ban imposed on him at Croydon Crown Court in 2011 following similar frauds. Previously he had used the name Mark Cas as well as Mark Castley and had got round the ban by changing his name by deed poll. He then cheated companies out of goods and services and defrauded two men who had applied to him for work.

One of the firms, Alford Technologies, which is a market leader in counter-explosive and IED (improvised explosive device) products and training, was defrauded of £27,000.

The judge said: 'I've got a psychologist's report on you and it talks about you as a man who thinks it may be important to be perceived as important, successful and wealthy. Your behaviour has all the hallmarks of a Walter Mitty character. In the fantasy world in which you live you think you are rich, you think you are successful. You are neither rich nor successful. Your forty-eight previous convictions show me you are completely unsuccessful in all that you do.'

The judge spared him jail, saying prison would be a waste of taxpayers' money because it had failed to stop him re-offending.

Handing down a two-year suspended sentence, the judge said: 'We are trying to stop you re-offending. I will impose a sentence that will appear to be light, but will give you the focus you need.'

It failed. Mrs Young handed over more that £14,000 to Buffett – then using his real name Mark Hill-Wood – but refused further requests for cash when he did not hand over dossiers detailing her ex-husband's assets he claimed to have retrieved. By then, Hill-Wood was living in a large detached house in Thames Ditton where he was arrested.

Michelle may have made the same mistake again. Perhaps she had a soft spot for con men. Just weeks before Scot Young died, she hired another private investigator to keep an eye on him. Fraud investigator Simon Sutton was the ninth private detective she had called in on the case. His company, Nevyan Intelligence Services, claimed to have more than twenty years' experience in fraud and corruption investigations across Europe, Asia, Western Africa, the Middle East and the Caribbean.

But Sutton, who lived with his wife and children in a modest £250,000 home in Hungerford, Berkshire, had a series of failed companies behind him and Nevyan was rated as 'high risk', having faced two county court judgements over debts amounting to over £4,500. According to Nevyan's website, the company required payment in advance for its services. However the *Daily Mail* found an online review from August 2012 that read: 'He takes hugely inflated fees hundred per cent in advance then delivers nothing. He is supposed to be a fraud investigator but uses that as a cover to rip customers off.'

While Michelle Young had courted the media, Scot had tried to stay out of the limelight, giving few interviews. But then Noelle Reno dragged him on to her reality-TV show *Ladies of London*. She admitted that he did not want to appear on the show.

'He is a very private person,' she said. 'You'll see on the show that he hates the cameras. Scot has spent his whole life paying people to keep him out of the press.'

At first, he refused to appear in the show, but Noelle feigned indifference.

'I said, "Fine, but you're not going to see me this summer." So he's in it. He hated every second.'

Scot was introduced on the show as 'Noelle's scandalous fiancé' and a man 'rumoured to be worth millions'. The papers said that the fact he agreed to appear on the show at all showed how much he loved her. Noelle also asserted that it spoke volumes about their relationship.

'You will see on the show that I wear the pants in our relationship,' she said. 'I've tried to date guys my age and I just steamroller them. My father says, "Why can't you just go find a nice banker with a Brooks Brothers shirt?" But I would get bored.'

Scot was filmed watching polo and talking about how contented he was feeling. They also searched for somewhere new to live together.

'The landlord gave us notice on our old flat because he was

moving back,' Noelle told the *Daily Telegraph* at Ladies' Day at Sandown Park.

But house-hunting was fraught with difficulties for this seemingly indecisive couple.

'The question is does one want to be in a house or a flat?' she said.

Scot was left in the driving seat for this one.

'I had to leave it to Scot to find us somewhere and we found our dream flat, but got outbid by JP Morgan,' said Noelle.

This was something of a comedown for a man who could once pull a £29-million mortgage.

In the first eight episodes, Scot was shown to live up to the high-maintenance blonde's demands, but failed to deliver. She said he was a shadow of the confident man she fell for due to his divorce battle.

'He's been stripped of his dignity and privacy,' she said.

In one heated scene in Selfridges department store in central London, she found out they were not moving into the new flat as planned. She told him: 'I need to know that when you say I'm taking care of this – you're the man. If not, I'm moving somewhere temporary and we'll re-evaluate.'

Scot begged her to keep her voice down, but she ordered him: 'Come through on what you say.'

There were other causes of friction. In one scene, he surprised her by plying her with champagne on the London Eye. She was unimpressed by this romantic gesture, saying: 'I hate heights and I'm claustrophobic.'

The romance seemed to be rocky too.

'We have been trying to get married for nearly four years and it still hasn't happened because of his divorce,' she said. 'Scot knows full stop that if he doesn't get this case sorted – I'm out of his life.'

Asked how she kept on smiling throughout it all, she said: 'How do you not? I guess I've learnt to detach to some extent.'

One fan was Noelle's aunt, Debra Lee Svinicki of Rio Verde, Arizona.

'I've watched *Ladies of London* a couple of times. I'm not the kind of person who watches those type of shows, but it's fun and it's fun to see Noelle,' she said. 'Noelle has had a lot of success over the last ten years.'

She also said that her niece had been 'very happy' with Mr Young. Plainly Noelle's remarks had not fallen on deaf ears. Despite his penury Scot had somehow managed to scrape together some cash and after they had finished filming he produced a six-carat diamond engagement ring and proposed. Rumours soon circulated that they were going go to get married in a lavish ceremony to be filmed for a TV fly-on-the-wall show the following year.

In the closing sequence of the show, the couple had moved home and Scot described how much they enjoyed living in Montagu Square.

'We are feeling settled, we love the area. It's great,' he said.

But not everything in the garden was rosy.

'It is up three flights of stairs with no lift,' Noelle complained. However, it was conveniently close to the Chiltern Firehouse, Marylebone's latest celebrity hangout. Otherwise, things were looking up.

'It has been a really tricky time this summer with the press,' said Noelle. 'Scot's divorce and me being dragged through that. But I can definitely see the light at the end of the tunnel. I am absolutely starting to realise that I need to be more strategic in my thinking and in my actions – a hundred per cent.'

It was from this flat that Scot Young plummeted to his death.

CHAPTER 18

UNSAVOURY CONNECTIONS

Within a day of Scot Young's untimely death, friends were telling the newspapers that they did not accept that he had committed suicide. While admitting that Young had been involved in a number of murky business deals, one friend told the *Daily Telegraph* that he 'questioned whether he would have taken his own life'. Clearly it was too early to tell.

A man in his thirties laying flowers by the railings where Young died said: 'We don't know what happened though, we don't know if it is suicide yet.'

A neighbour said: 'I was not at home when he died but I was told there had been a row in that flat on that day'.

Another resident told the *Times*: 'It was rumoured he had fallen out with his girlfriend' and another said she had been there earlier on the day he died.

One insider told the *Evening Standard*: 'I think the on-going divorce caused a lot of friction and difficulty and I think maybe that's what has come between them.'

But there were rumours that 'he was also forging relationships with less savoury characters, including members of the Russian underworld'. During the divorce battle one British businessman told friends he had severed ties with Young because he had become a 'bag man for the mafia'.

An anonymous friend has claimed Project Moscow was a scam – not one used by Young to siphon off money so he would not have to pay Michelle, but one conducted by the Russian mafia to fleece British businessmen. Speaking to the *Daily Telegraph*, the source said the deal was orchestrated by Berezovsky, who believed it to be genuine. He was now dead. It also involved two other developers, Paul Castle and Robert Curtis, both of whom had died in mysterious circumstances. Under the terms of the deal, the three put up £140 million, but were then lent the same amount again by other Russians to double the deposit. When the Russian government pulled the plug, not only was all the money lost but the businessmen owed tens of millions to the Russian mafia, who began to hound them.

The High Court was told that Mr Young had bought a 50 per cent share of Project Moscow for £12 million from Ruslan Fomichev, business partner of Boris Berezovsky. He had also raised $18 million from investors including Ekaterina Berezovskaya, the oligarch's daughter, and Poju Zabludowicz. But they were saying nothing.

If there was any connection to the Russian mafia, it would have most likely come through Berezovsky. After he lost his lawsuit against Abramovich, he told family members that he feared that he had been poisoned. His daughter Elizaveta Berezovskaya said her father told her 'something strange was happening to him' and 'some chemical reaction was inside him'.

There were other suspicious deaths surrounding the deal. Stephen Curtis, the lawyer said to have introduced Young, Castle and Robert Curtis to the Russians, died in a helicopter crash in 2004 after telling friends he thought his life was in danger. Another businessman with links to Young named Johnny Elichaoff – ex-husband of Trinny Woodall, of Trinny and Susannah fame – fell to his death from the roof of Whiteley shopping centre in London just one month before Young died.

Although all these deaths may indeed be suicides or accidents, the suggestion was those involved were being intimidated. It was claimed Young had been dangled by his legs out of the window of the Dorchester Hotel on Park Lane by gangsters in 2012. Several people said Young told them he feared for his life.

'I do not believe for one minute Scot committed suicide,' the friend told the *Daily Telegraph*. 'My heart tells me he was killed. There is no way he would have jumped to his death. I knew him very, very well, we have been friends for over twenty years. We are all very scared about what might happen. Two years ago he was hung off the balcony of a hotel room at the Dorchester by Russian mafia he owed money to, before he went to prison. He never went back there after that. I believe Scot was murdered.'

The reason? 'He owed a lot of money to the wrong sort of people. I'm absolutely devastated. He was a really nice guy.'

Other friends confirmed that Scot had expressed fears for his safety only a month before his death.

'He was very worried, he said he knew someone was following him,' he said. 'Many of Scot's friends aren't surprised that he died.'

He even told one friend that he felt safer in Pentonville.

'In many ways prison life was easier,' he had said. 'Despite being locked up with murderers, rapists and drug dealers, I actually felt safe – that nobody could touch me.'

Again, the friend said Scot 'owed cash to the wrong people'.

Friends admitted that Young had suffered mental instability while the divorce was going on. But Noelle was making Scot happy and he was on the road to recovery after going through a bleak time.

One said: 'He was suffering from depression but he would not have done this. He was truly in love with Noelle, he had asked her to marry him and they were going to wed next year. He idolised her. She wasn't with him for the money. He would have done anything for her.'

However, there were also rumours that the couple had split up in the weeks before he died and the engagement was off. A friend of Noelle's told the *Daily Mail*: 'We are all wondering whether he [Scot] was pushed – or even told he had to jump. There was a lot of pressure on him recently. We didn't know exactly why but there were a lot of arguments... They called off the engagement a few weeks ago but they were still seeing each other... I just don't see him committing suicide.'

In recent years, it was known he had attempted suicide, spent time in rehab and had been sectioned twice. A neighbour said: 'He was drinking a lot. It seemed like the wheels were starting to come off.'

But James Creed had spoken to Young minutes before his death and had no inkling that anything was wrong.

'It's unbelievable, just shocking,' he said. 'How can a man die like that? It doesn't make sense does it? I knew Scot well. We did everything together. I spoke to him on the phone on Monday, it must have been at around four in the afternoon.

UNSAVOURY CONNECTIONS

I suppose that means I was the last person to talk to him. He seemed quiet, nothing unusual. No one would have expected this. When I heard it I felt miserable. He was a great man, really wonderful.'

Later he admitted that Scot was not his usual outgoing self.

'He was quiet, which wasn't like him. He seemed distracted but didn't say anything unusual,' said Creed. 'I can't believe he committed suicide but there was a lot of pressure on him. He was under too much pressure and people do things when they are not thinking straight.'

He pooh-poohed claims his friend had been killed or threatened by Russian gangsters because of his links with the tycoon Boris Berezovsky or through his other business dealings.

'If Scot had been dangled out of a window, I would know about it,' said Creed. 'I spoke to him on the phone every day and saw him at least once a week. No one knew Scot better than me. There will always be speculation because of the divorce case and because he sold his house to Boris and because Boris was involved in Project Moscow, but that is what it is, speculation.'

While rumours were flying, more bouquets were turning up where the section of railings removed by firefighters had been. Young was well known in the area. Twenty-one-year-old Shahab Awan who worked nearby and laid a bunch of flowers outside the Marylebone flat said: 'He was my mentor, he taught me so much about business. Keep grafting, that's what he told me. He was a great guy and he had a great business manner. This death is a shock to lots of people in Marylebone. He was always so friendly and jokey. I heard about it and felt so shocked. I spent a whole day thinking and talking about him. I heard that Noelle had said that he was very fond of me. She is obviously very upset about this terrible tragedy at the moment.'

Another bouquet carried a message that read: 'Scott: From all the boys in Miami and home, miss you, love you, see you in the next life! Nin, April, Hannah, Jade, Bob, Bish, Tony, Wayne and Jonny.'

One more said: 'To Scott. Miss you mate and love you dearly, hope peace has been found and you know I have your back while you have left us. Jonathan B.'

Debra Lee Svinicki, sister-in-law of Noelle's mother Carole Anne, was, again, left to speak for the family.

'I'm very shocked at this tragedy,' she said. 'I'm sure Noelle must be very upset. The family will rally around Noelle. Carole is very close to Noelle, she visits her as often as she can. I don't know how close she is to Scot. I just know that she [Noelle] was very happy with him.'

The family's plans were now all awry.

'At Christmas we expect to see Noelle, but we don't know now because this has happened,' said her aunt who lived in a desert community just outside Phoenix, Arizona. 'I have no idea if she will stay in London or what she will do next.'

Naturally, the controversy over Scot Young's death trended on twitter. Duncan Bannatyne, millionaire star of BBC Two's *Dragon's Den*, joined the sceptics.

'Jeeesus Christ. Just read Scot Young is dead. I don't believe he killed himself. Killed by despicable family lawyers more like,' he tweeted. Bannatyne had also been involved in an acrimonious divorce case that reportedly cost him £345 million, leaving him with just £85 million. He added: 'Scot died after being dragged thro family courts for 7 yrs. He was a good man.'

However, in 2013, Bannatyne said that he considered suicide after his own divorce case.

Even forensic investigator L. Burke Files, part of a team Mrs

Young called in to probe her husband's finances during his divorce battle, said there was 'no way' he jumped to his death.

'The sort of man who prefers to go to jail instead of telling the court about his finances isn't the sort of man who chucks himself out of windows,' he said.

Young's friends also linked his death to those of Paul Castle and Robert Curtis, who had once dated the model Caprice.

'All owed a lot of money to the wrong people,' one said. 'I think they have been murdered or forced to take themselves out.'

Young's business associate, George Constantine, was said to have 'disappeared' shortly after giving evidence during Mr Young's divorce case. Friends of Mr Constantine, who once looked after Young's property portfolio, said he has not been seen for months and had changed his phone number. In court he admitted that in 2011 £80,000 had been paid into his bank account by people he had never met. He had then handed it on to Mr Young. It was suggested that he had gone into hiding, rather than joining what the press was now calling the Ring of Death.

Like Young, Robert Curtis had made a fortune in the London property market and enjoyed a jet-set lifestyle with a fleet of expensive cars and a wardrobe full of designer clothes. He made his fortune in letting up-market properties in the early 2000s from his St John's Wood headquarters and travelled in a chauffeur-driven Rolls-Royce with a personalised number plate.

He knew Scot Young through his business dealings and the pair were said to have been friends who met regularly in London restaurants. His business empire fell apart during the recession and he was left struggling under huge debts. At his height he was a director of fifteen firms. Only one remained at the time of his death and according to a close friend, it was rumoured to owe more than half-a-million to the Turkish mafia.

His former accountant, Anthony Morris, described him as a 'cavalier, ebullient' businessman who was a 'mover and shaker' who 'made tons of money and spent it'.

Used to living the 'high life', Curtis was renowned for attending parties around the world. But he had been forced to move in with his parents prior to his death, though his final address was the Travelodge in Whetstone, North London. The father of one, he died after falling under a south-bound train at Kingsbury Underground station after an excess of cocaine and painkillers in December 2012. He was forty-seven.

The inquest ruled that his death was suicide. On his body were a photograph of him and his daughter with the words 'I love you baby xxx' written on the back, along with a note saying 'I love you mum and dad' with his father's phone number written on it. It was also said that he been badly affected by the suicide of fellow property entrepreneur Paul Castle two years earlier.

A self-made businessman, Castle had died in November 2010, also under the wheels of an Underground train. He was fifty-four when he died. A friend of the Prince of Wales, he was said to be a polo 'legend', though he only started playing in the early 1990s. He was photographed shaking hands with the Queen after one match. In 1997, he achieved notoriety when he was fined £5,000 and banned from playing polo for nine months for 'abuse of the stick' after hitting an opponent over the head with a wooden mallet at the Guards Polo Club.

At one time Castle owned a private plane, a Ferrari and a Bentley, while his property empire stretched across England, France and Switzerland. But it was said that he was experiencing severe financial difficulties due to the collapse of the property market in the run-up to his death. He was also forced to close his Michelin-starred restaurant called The Goose in Britwell Salome, near Watlington, Oxfordshire. He also had problems with his health but, prior to his death, insisted to his doctor that he was not depressed. He had been due to marry for the fourth time to his fiancée Natalie Theo, a former fashion editor he lived with in London and Berkshire.

Castle was caught on CCTV entering the Bond Street Underground station before jumping in front of a train with, it was said, 'his hands outstretched as if diving'. Westminster coroner Dr Paul Knapman concluded the death was suicide.

'Things were not going well and it appears that he decided, probably on impulse, to end his own life,' Knapman said.

Their friend Johnny Elichaoff was a former antiques dealer and as previously mentioned the ex-husband of the television presenter Trinny Woodall. He was fifty-five when he died in November 2014 after falling from the roof of Whiteleys shopping centre in West London.

He had started out in the 1970s as a rock drummer. With the bands Stark Naked and the Car Thieves, he toured the world supporting bands such as U2. In the mid-1980s he spent two years completing his national service in Israel before returning to the music business as manager for acts including Tears for Fears and Fairground Attraction. Then he moved into finance, as a life insurance and inheritance tax adviser. It was through his finance work that he is thought to have met Scot Young and the two of them became good friends.

He moved into television as an antiques expert on the Channel Four show *Four Rooms* where members of the public tried to sell valuable or collectable items and he married Ms Woodall, from the BBC's *What Not To Wear*, in 1999. They divorced ten years later.

After breaking his leg in a motorcycle accident – leading to twenty operations – he became addicted to prescription painkillers and in 2006 sought treatment in a Californian rehab clinic. Falling on hard times, he was forced to sell his businesses and was thought to have been talked down from the roof of Whiteley's just weeks before he died. Friends said they were devastated, but could not understand why he would have wanted to take his own life.

With Young and Berezovsky, these high-fliers enjoyed regular nights out in some of London's finest restaurants and there was a rivalry between them.

'Scot and his pals were always trying to outdo each other,' a friend said. 'It was all about who has the biggest yacht, the fastest car. It's money and power.'

By the beginning of December 2014, Young was the only one of them left alive.

Berezovsky's inquest had been held in Windsor Guildhall nine months earlier. It was told that the oligarch had been discovered in the bathroom of his former home in Berkshire with a ligature around his neck. He was sixty-seven. Thames Valley Police had investigated the possibility that there had been foul play, but detectives said they found no sign of a struggle.

Home Office pathologist Dr Simon Poole, who carried out a post-mortem examination, said there was nothing to indicate any other people were involved. There was also no evidence to suggest Berezovsky was poisoned, according to investigations by toxicologists.

However, Professor Bernd Brinkmann, a German forensic scientist who dealt with hanging and asphyxiation cases, brought in by Berezovsky's family, said his examination had led him to conclude that the oligarch had not taken his own life. The marks on Berezovsky's neck could not have come from hanging, he said. They were 'far away from the typical inverse V shape' usually seen. The congestion to Berezovsky's face was also not consistent with hanging. It was more likely he had been strangled by someone else and then hanged from the shower rail in the bathroom.

The coroner Peter Bedford said: 'You conclude that you believe that this was a strangulation by a third party.'

However he warned Dr Brinkmann against going into the 'realms of speculation' when he said he believed two people were involved.

Berezovsky's daughter Elizaveta Berezovskaya told the inquest she feared he was assassinated for warning that Vladimir Putin was a 'danger to the world'.

'He was a target, always,' she said. 'My father was a very serious political figure.'

Initially, she and the family had accepted that her father's death was suicide, but 'the more I thought about it, the more doubts I had'.

The Berkshire coroner said he had heard 'compelling evidence' to suggest that Mr Berezovsky had been depressed and was under immense financial pressure but, having heard conflicting expert evidence about how he was found hanging, recorded an open verdict.

Russia has denied its secret services were involved in his death, but Putin said that he could not rule out Western intelligence playing a role, though he admitted he had no such evidence.

Berezovsky had drawn up a new will nine days before his death, but not one of the executors was prepared to take up the job. Those involved said that his estate would take years to unscramble.

Ex-wives Nina Korotkova and Galina Besharova, long-time partner Yelena Gorbunova and his latest lover Katerina Sabirova, along with Chechen exile Akhmed Zakayev, were all seen at the graveside.

CHAPTER 19

AND THEN
THERE WERE NONE

Boris Berezovsky was behind Project Moscow, which Scot Young and his friends invested in. It had collapsed, costing all those involved hundreds of millions of pounds – and possibly their lives. At the beginning of December 2014, only one of them was left alive. And then, on 8 December, there were none.

'All five men moved in the same circles and would regularly enjoy nights out at some of London's finest restaurants,' said a friend to the *Daily Telegraph*, maintaining anonymity because he feared for his life. 'There were five friends who all ate together at Cipriani [now called C London] who are all now dead. They were all linked in business and all owed a lot of money to the wrong people.'

The five were Scot Young, Boris Berezovsky, Robert Curtis, Paul Castle and Johnny Elichaoff. Soon a sixth name was being added to the Ring of Death. It was that of Stephen Curtis, a lawyer who allegedly introduced Young, Paul Castle, Robert Curtis and Johnny Elichaoff to his Russian contacts. He died when his new £1.5-million Agusta 109 helicopter crashed a mile from Bournemouth airport in 2004. The pilot Max Radford was also killed. The coroner recorded a verdict of accidental death on both men after the pilot lost his bearings in bad weather. But a friend of Stephen Curtis's was not so sure.

'He was in a brand new helicopter, on a trip from Battersea which he did regularly to his castle in Dorset with an experienced pilot,' the unnamed pal of Stephen Curtis said. 'It was no accident. He had told friends he feared he would be killed just weeks before.'

A week before the fatal crash, Curtis was said to have told a friend: 'If anything happens to me in the next few weeks, it will not be an accident.'

His uncle told the inquest his nephew had received threatening phone calls and been under some kind of surveillance before his death. Unsurprisingly, Stephen Curtis was also an associate of Boris Berezovsky.

Stephen Curtis's friend claimed thick layers of 'whitewash' had also been painted over the other deaths.

'They are all good people,' the source said. 'There is no doubt some of them did commit suicide. But people should not be allowed to go around bullying my friends into killing themselves. Scot had been a broken man over the last few years but they were all caught up with very, very nasty people. Paul Castle was so frightened. They visited him and he handed over his whole watch collection to appease them. They said if he did not pay up he would be killed, not by a shot to the head but in a slow nasty way. He then went straight to Bond Street Station and killed himself.'

He said that, in 2011, Robert Curtis told him he owed some

'messy people' a lot of money. A year later, he was dead. Another friend confirmed that Young, Castle and Curtis had produced at least £140 million between them to put into Project Moscow.

'They were asked for the money but were then offered a quasi-deal whereby other Russians lent them more money to put in as a deposit, as a loan,' he said. 'The original sum was matched again. So they are now in it to the tune of at least £280 million and are already in debt. But then the so-called planners in the Russian government pulled the plug. Where did the money go? That is the question.'

Robert Curtis was convinced they had been set up, the source said. But there were indications that the whole thing was a 'sting operation' to entrap Berezovsky. Young and his accomplices were badly burned. Along the way leading figures in the Russian mafia were also said to have lost heavily.

Max Radford's mother was also convinced that her son's death was no accident.

'It was no pilot error – that is balderdash,' she said.

At the time, Stephen Curtis was working for Russian oligarch Mikhail Khodorkovsky – a billionaire oil magnate and enemy of Vladimir Putin who was jailed in 2003 on fraud charges. Amnesty International said his conviction was politically motivated.

Max Radford's mother Gloria said: 'I know Putin wanted these oligarchs because they got so much of the country's money. Stephen Curtis was helping them to get their money invested in the tax havens. Real answers lie in Russia.'

Asked if she thought Putin's supporters were able to have his enemies murdered in the UK, she said: 'Yes, I wouldn't be surprised.' His father thought the helicopter had been downed by a bomb.

Their lawyer son, who was worth £100 million and lived in a Dorset Castle, was certainly in fear for his life. He moved his desk away from the window of his London office and hired a bodyguard. It was thought that he had begged the Foreign Office and National Crime Intelligence Service for help, allegedly offering to shop other Russian oligarchs for crimes in return for protection after being plagued by death threats.

In one menacing phone call, a man with a Russian accent mentioned his wife Sarah and thirteen-year-old daughter. Another call, also from a Russian, warned: 'We are here. We are behind you. We follow you.'

Stephen Curtis's uncle Eric said: 'He had approached people he believed were watching him and offered them a cup of tea.'

Dennis Radford, father of the dead pilot, condemned the official report into the crash as a 'whitewash'. Of the real answers, he said: 'We believe they lie in what was going on in Russia at that time.'

Mrs Radford wanted an open verdict at the inquest.

'I want to say a lot more, but I'm afraid I can't,' she told the *Express on Sunday*. 'It is fair to say a lot of significant things haven't come into play.'

While others were seeking justice – or, at least, some plausible reason why their nearest and dearest were dead – Mrs Young was still looking for the money. A source close to Michelle said: 'It remains to be seen if anything can be found now he is dead. Someone somewhere knows something but isn't saying.'

It seems unlikely that she will ever collect though. The bankruptcy trustee David Ingram told the *Sun*: 'Whilst Scot is now dead, he remains bankrupt, albeit deceased. This will pose problems, not least of which is a proposal that we were discussing whereby Michelle would be paid the entirety of her claim over five years from Scot's future earnings. Clearly this can no longer happen.'

The former Scotland Yard officer who worked as a private investigator for Michelle Young urged the police to examine Mr Young's laptops, mobile phones and computers thoroughly for clues that might unlock the riddle of death.

'Mr Young was incredibly careful about what he wrote on his computers,' he said. 'We had a look at one laptop and there was nothing significant. However, when we went into the deleted files there was a lot of interesting material.'

Scot Young was so paranoid about security he would delete his computer files as soon as he had used them.

'It seemed that he printed off important information and deleted it quickly,' said the detective. 'He also liked to keep a lot of information in his head. Although the Yard are not treating his death as suspicious, they should go through his computers, particularly the deleted files.'

Friends of Scot Young urged the police to open a murder investigation. It was clearly a possibility that Stephen Curtis, Scot Young and the rest of the Ring of Death had been rubbed out by Russian hit men after Project Moscow backfired, earning them a string of enemies.

Oxford University professor Federico Varese, author of *The Russian Mafia*, said: 'Whether Mr Young's death was a professional hit, I guess you'd have to keep an open mind. He had attempted suicide before. The mafia have, however, used hit men in London – when a Russian banker was gunned down a few years ago in Docklands. Russians are increasingly investing in London because there is a lot of flexibility in the financial system and their money is safe.'

By 2014 there were thought to be more than 150,000 Russians living in London, often dubbed Londongrad or Moscow-on-

Thames. With the collapse of the rouble, more were on their way and Russian mafia bosses were thought to be moving in on London's vice trade, threatening pimps, taking over escort services or massage parlours and using eastern European prostitutes in small brothels in Soho.

Stewart Lansley, co-author of *Londongrad: From Russia With Cash*, agreed. He told the *Sunday Mail* that the circumstances of the deaths, when taken together, merited further investigation.

'The whole world of Russian emigrés and oligarchs has always been surrounded by mystery and intrigue,' he said. 'There have been a number of strange incidents. These deaths may well be a series of unfortunate accidents. But it seems there are so many of these accidents within these circles that it does raise question marks – and this is something you do feel needs looking into. If it was just a one-off, even two or three, that may be relatively normal. But it's more than that – it's five or six, at least – and this does raise questions.'

He said he had spent a lot of time investigating the death of Stephen Curtis and had still never really got to the bottom of it. He also pointed out the dangers of mass immigration of rich Russians to those who dealt with them.

'The Russians arrived, started moving their money in, bringing their children here and buying property,' he said. There was a whole entourage who they met, employed and used – those who provided property and financial services and so on.

'These included the likes of Stephen Curtis and it appears Scot Young was involved, too. These people played a supporting role and made a huge amount of money in the process. I called them the British bag carriers for the oligarchs – and quite a few have ended up dead. It's absolutely possible that these were all genuine accidents but it is an intriguing set of circumstances.'

AND THEN THERE WERE NONE

With the exception of Berezovsky, those in the Ring of Death were not used to dealing with the type of people they were doing business with in Russia.

'Mr Young certainly lost a lot of money and by all accounts it was something to do with some kind of dodgy dealing involving Russia,' he said. 'You carry high risks getting involved with these people. Most have done very well without any problems but there has been this string of five or six people who have died in circumstances we will probably never get to the bottom of. Mr Young lost a lot of money, ended up in jail, was suffering from depression and is reported to have been having problems with his girlfriend so it's possible it got the better of him and he has taken his own life. But we know this mafia-like Russian oligarch world is full of vendettas, deep-seated financial feuds and political intrigue. Anybody that gets involved with them does walk a tightrope – and there's always a risk that you'll fall off the tightrope.'

Another writer familiar with the mindset of Russian oligarchs advised anyone seeking an answer to the mystery of Young's death to 'follow the money'.

'Why was he so desperate not to reveal the details of his assets and their origins to the British courts?' asked the writer. 'What did he fear would happen if he did so?'

According to the *Sunday Telegraph*: 'New sources, too scared to be named, began to come forward on an almost daily basis to claim that the deaths were neither suicide nor accident.'

There was talk of the involvement of the Turkish mafia, as well as that of the Russian variety. The newspaper quoted Akhmed Zakayev, who is painfully aware of the violence, greed and corruption in Russian business and politics that followed the collapse of the Soviet Union.

'It all looks suspicious and most likely there is a connection between these deaths,' he said.

While Zakayev would not comment more specifically on the death of Scot Young and his immediate associates, he said he remained convinced that the death of Boris Berezovsky, like those of others who have crossed Putin, was not the case of a desperate man taking his own life.

'It was not a suicide,' he said. 'I am not the only one with these views. The fact the judge could not decide whether it was suicide or not makes me believe even more that Mr Berezovsky in fact did not kill himself.'

The questions were being asked inside Russia too. State-run Vesti FM said that Young's death was 'a very unusual and extraordinarily interesting story'. It was not the only one asking bluntly: 'Did he fall or was he thrown?'

But why was a state-run Russian radio station interested in the apparent suicide of an English businessman nearly two thousand miles away in London?

'It was found out that within recent months, Scot Young told his close friends that his life was in danger and somebody wanted to kill him,' the station said. 'The friends who talk about a violent death are linking this to the demise of Boris Berezovsky.'

The Kremlin's official newspaper *Rossiyskaya Gazeta* made another connection. It named Young's business partner Ruslan Fomichev as part of a joint scheme 'to invest in a development project on the grounds of a former paint factory in Moscow'.

It stressed that Fomichev was close to Berezovsky. They had worked together for nineteen years – from the time Berezovsky had been a Kremlin insider. Young, of course, was a member of Berezovsky's inner circle. Fomichev had also left Russia and moved to London, but later he had fallen out with Berezovsky in a business dispute.

Fomichev was thought to have been close to another of Putin's enemies – Alexander Litvinenko. After Litvinenko's death in 2006, Fomichev was interviewed by Russian investigators in London, according to accounts in Moscow. He was also a regular on the party scene in London. His glamorous wife Ekaterina featured in *Tatler* and was a close friend of socialite Tamara Beckwith. A Russian gossip columnist said Ekaterina – also known as Katia – was the person to tell Roman Abramovich's first wife Irina that he was seeing Dasha Zhukova, prompting their multi-million-pound divorce.

Though Fomichev was based in London, he maintained active Russian business interests and had close ties to the oil-rich region of Bashkortostan, which some sources say he represents in London.

The newspaper lined up others to firm up the connection. A female friend of Young's was quoted: 'The police must think about Young's friendship with the oligarch Boris Berezovsky. Police must pay attention to this and remember the death of Boris Berezovsky.'

Russian reports stressed that Young was in Berezovsky's 'closest circle'.

One said: 'A rich pal of the late Boris Berezovsky, Scot Young, committed suicide, according to London police. Let us remind you that Boris Berezovsky also committed suicide last year, and in mysterious circumstances. One of the theories is that he hanged himself.'

But it was not just official Kremlin sources that were interested in Scot Young's death. The 'independent' web source Svodka.net said that Young's death could be linked to the rush to secure assets amid the economic crisis in Russia caused by falling oil prices and Western sanctions, though it gave no further details. The former tycoon's death coincided with a catastrophic fall in the rouble.

'The British millionaire did not survive the Russian crisis,' said Svodka.net. 'One of the richest people in the UK has fallen out of his window in London. Businessman Scot Young was a friend of Boris Berezovsky. Police excludes the idea of murder, but the friends and colleagues of the dead man do not believe he committed suicide. According to them, Scot Young lost his fortune buying property in Moscow. He had debts of many millions. But according to other information, Young was not bankrupt. He had just hidden his wealth off-shore.'

Despite the allegations of Russian mafia involvement, no one gave the names of his gangland links. Even friends of Mrs Young were concerned about the Berezovksy link.

'Michelle doesn't know where the money is and now he is no longer here,' said a female friend. 'It is possible we may never know where it has gone. The police need to look at this and the death of Boris Berezovsky again. At first glance they appear to have a lot in common.'

Another close friend, who has known the Youngs since before their marriage, said she could not believe he would ever take his own life. She said it has always been unclear where his huge wealth came from and described many of the stories given during the High Court battle as 'myths'.

Intriguingly, the friend said that when Young was at the centre of a police inquiry in the late 1990s, at one stage he was being hunted by a helicopter. While Young was not convicted of any offence, he claimed he had been confronted by a plain-clothes police officer who said: 'I will get you one day.'

CHAPTER 20

CLOSER TO HOME

Scot Young may also have had more trouble closer to home. Just weeks before his death, his ex-wife challenged him about his links to the Adams family, still one of the country's most notorious crime gangs, thought to be worth £200 million. She said she believed that some of her ex-husband's money might have come from organised crime and the Adams family had been linked to drug trafficking, money laundering and murder. She reminded the newspapers that his links to key members of the Adams family had been investigated by the police in the early years of their relationship. He had been close to the enforcer Patsy Adams who had been convicted of armed robbery in the 1970s.

Since Scot Young had first been associated with the Adams Family in the 1990s, the A-Team had not been sitting still. They had formed international links with various criminal organizations, particularly Latin American drug cartels and in their home territory they seemed to operate with impunity. The failure of the authorities to make charges stick against some members of the gang had led to them gaining the reputation of being 'untouchables'. They allegedly worked with Jamaican Yardie gangs to silence informants and neutralise rivals.

'They created fear just through their name, and undoubtedly a lot of violence was carried out on their behalf,' said Wensley Clarkson.

Cases never got off the ground or collapsed. Juries, it seemed, were regularly nobbled. Whenever gang members came to court, even court officials were provided with twenty-four-hour police protection. But the Adamses had grown up on the streets. Young coppers who had their palms greased over minor matters in the old days back in Islington had now risen in the Metropolitan Police Force. It has been alleged that some senior detectives remained on the payroll. That, it has been suggested, is why the Adams family managed to develop an uncanny ability to second-guess police surveillance operations.

'Listening devices go dead, their plans are mysteriously changed and word drifts back that they know what we're up to,' one retired detective told Wensley Clarkson.

Their influence knew no bounds. Mark Herbert, a clerk with the Crown Prosecution Service, was convicting of selling the Adams family, through an intermediary, the names of thirty-three informants in return for £500. Admitting that he knew he was signing the informants' death warrants, Herbert said: 'They will send them flowers, but not possibly for their birthdays.' Herbert knew exactly who he was dealing with in the Adams family. His father was a policeman.

When HM Customs & Excise and the Inland Revenue took a

look, they discovered that the Adamses had no bank accounts, no tax records and did not even own the houses they lived in. As far as the state bureaucracy was concerned, they did not exist. In the late 1990s, when they had time off from stopping IRA terrorism and Soviet subversion, MI5 was employed to investigate the Adamses. Its officers are said to have bugged Adamses' homes and cars and followed them closely over a period of several years, working in tandem with both the newly created National Crime Squad and the National Criminal Intelligence Agency, as well as the Inland Revenue.

Like the Krays before them, the Adamses cultivated friends in high places. In 1996 one Tory MP came under close scrutiny by detectives and MI5 agents trying to break the family's stranglehold on London's West End clubland. The politician was even rumoured to own a private company that supplied the Adams family with an arsenal of weapons smuggled out of former Eastern bloc countries including sub-machine guns.

In the summer of 1997, the A-Team spread a rumour that they had donated thousands of pounds to the Labour Party just before the party's historic landslide victory over the Tories in the same year. It was a coincidence, of course, that Tony Blair was also a resident of Islington. Tommy Adams told associates he made several payments to the party through two henchmen, Michael Papamichael and Edward Wilkinson, both later jailed for gang-related offences. But since gifts of less than £5,000 do not have to be publicly disclosed by political parties, no record of them has ever been discovered.

However, unlike the Krays, the Adamses did not hanker for a high-profile lifestyle. This would further draw attention to their activities. They steered clear of most of their club interests in the West End and hid themselves away in a small number of old North London haunts which they knew could be trusted – or on the Costa del Sol. But they kept fit and dressed stylishly, like the football players, boxers and other minor celebrities they hung out with.

The A-Team also invested a lot of their dirty money in the world of horse racing through horse race fixer Brian Wright, also known as 'The Milkman' because he always delivered. He had a box at the Royal Ascot race meeting for fourteen years and was a member of the exclusive clubs Tramps and Annabels in London.

When detectives raided his luxury apartment in Chelsea Harbour, West London, not far from some of the A-Team's most profitable West London clubs, he was unexpectedly away at his £2 million villa named El Lechero, the Spanish for The Milkman, near Marbella. It was close to the Costa Del Sol's biggest horse-racing track.

Business dealings with Wright had not always gone smoothly. On one occasion, two high-ranking Adams enforcers were arrested on their way to resolve a dispute involving the same man. They were armed.

Through Wright, the A-Team was thought to have forged close connections to jockeys and bookmakers involved in race-fixing. The Adamses made huge profits from betting on horse racing, investing in properties in London and the home counties with six-figure cheques from well-known bookmakers.

In 1996, Wright's yacht *Sea Mist* was boarded by Irish Police in Cork Harbour. They found 1,230 pounds of cocaine hidden in the dumb waiter. The gangster awaiting the shipment in Hampshire left behind Wright's Channel 4 Racing Diary containing contact numbers for other members of his cartel, as well as dozens of famous names in horse racing and TV.

In 1997, police began bugging his flat in Chelsea Harbour and following him and his friends. He was arrested on race-fixing charges. After he was released on bail, he fled to Spain.

The following year his son was arrested in connection with the smuggling investigation. Wright paid £20,000 through his daughter Joanne for a private jet to take him to Northern Cyprus, which has no extradition treaty.

Wright senior was arrested in Spain in 2005 and flown back to Britain to face trial. Associates faced money laundering charges. Wright was sentenced to thirty years for drug smuggling. He was estimated to be worth £600 million, but refused to attend hearings that aimed to claw back the proceeds of his crimes, figuring that, at sixty-one, he was going to die in prison anyway.

The case against Tommy Adams in September 1998 was one of the few successful prosecutions against family members in their ongoing war with Scotland Yard. He was arrested in a London hotel shortly after police seized cannabis worth £250,000 brought from Thailand and Turkey hidden in cargos of garlic.

Fearing that he might be under surveillance, Tommy carried out his negotiations in the back of a taxi. But it had been bugged, along with his hotel room. Over nine months the police built up a catalogue of evidence against him, including knowledge of the .44 Magnum that he kept hidden in a flowerpot in his £450,000 place in King's Cross.

Adams, who lived most of the time in Spain to thwart police operations, admitted cannabis trafficking after a series of legal negotiations. He was jailed for seven-and-a-half years and was ordered to pay £1 million from the profits within a year or serve another five years in jail. When Tommy was taken down to start his sentence, he was chewing gum and laughing. His wife Androulla paid just two days before the deadline.

Michael Papamichael and Edward Wilkinson, two friends of Tommy's from school days, also pleaded guilty to drug charges. Papamichael was jailed for six years and Wilkinson was sentenced to a total of nine years for cannabis and cocaine trafficking.

Maybe the police did not just get lucky in this case. It was rumoured that the rest of the A-Team had 'allowed' the prosecution to go through to teach wildman Tommy a lesson because he'd been setting up drug deals behind the backs of the rest of the family. However, detectives said that the Adams family – also known as The Firm – operated like a major company with a number of senior directors who ran their own enterprises.

Just three months after Tommy Adams had gone down, diamond merchant Solly Nahome was gunned down outside his North London home. A professional hit man pumped four bullets into him before escaping on a waiting motorcycle. It was a classic Adams hit. With an office in Hatton Garden, Nahome was a specialist in fraud and money laundering, as well as being the A-Team's trusted financial adviser. Recruited by Patsy, he was said to have met with members of the Adams family two or three times a week and arranged for £25 million to be hidden in property deals and off-shore accounts.

Like other characters associated with the Adams family, Nahome tried to live anonymously. His address does not appear on the electoral register and he preferred to pay for everything in cash. The cash-only environment of Hatton Garden was the perfect place for laundering drugs money. It emerged that one of Osama bin Laden's top lieutenants had visited Hatton Garden in the run-up to the 9/11 attacks to raise funds for al-Qaeda.

Before his death, Nahome is said to have been on a number of trips abroad, including one visit to Israel, for business deals connected with the Adams family. He also opened a bar-restaurant near Hatton Garden as a front for their interests.

At first, police suspected that this was the first shot in a gangland war to unseat the Adamses. Soon after the hit Patsy flew home. But there was no reason to think that the Adamses had lost their grip.

In May 1999, they were given another opportunity to demonstrate their invincibility in criminal courts when police decided to prosecute them over another case centring on money laundering. Patsy Adams's golfing partner, forty-four-year-old Chris McCormack, was charged with grievous bodily harm with intent. The victim was David McKenzie, a wealthy forty-six-year-old financier with an office in Mayfair. McKenzie laundered drug money for the Adams family, but those investments took a nose-dive and he lost close to £1.5 million of the A-Team's money.

McKenzie was invited to Terry Adams' mansion in Mill Hill, North London, to discuss the situation. He was left in no doubt that the money had to be recouped. A few days later, when the cash was not forthcoming, McKenzie said he was summoned to another meeting, this time at the Islington home of Adams's brother-in-law John Potter. There, the prosecution said, McCormack set about McKenzie. He was kicked and beaten, sustaining three broken ribs. Then it was said that McCormack carved him up with a Stanley knife to the point where just fragments of skin were keeping his nose and left ear attached to his face. Two tendons on his left wrist were severed, permanently affecting the use of his hand. According to one detective, the attack left him with more lines than a map of the London Underground. When McKenzie finally took the stand at the Old Bailey trial, there were audible gasps of shock.

'They'd cut him to ribbons,' said one observer.

McKenzie described the first meeting with Terry Adams, who was acknowledged as 'the chief exec of the Adams family board'. There was no doubt that he was the boss.

'Everyone stood up when he walked in,' McKenzie said. 'He looked like a star... a cross between Liberace and Peter Stringfellow. He was immaculately dressed, in a long black coat and white frilly shirt. He was totally in command.'

On the outside, Terry Adams's discreetly guarded but substantial North London mansion bristled with CCTV cameras, radar beam alarms and six-inch thick bullet-proof windows. Inside it was tastefully decorated and filled with antique furniture and expensive objets d'art. He is a well-mannered man of cultured tastes, with a liking for good wine and custom-built cars.

When Potter gave evidence during the trial, he accepted that McKenzie had been injured at his home, but maintained that the attacker was a complete stranger. The police were not impressed by this story. Nevertheless, he was cleared of committing acts intended to pervert the course of justice.

McCormack admitted meeting McKenzie three times to recover the debt 'as a favour to my old mate Patsy'. DNA samples of McKenzie's blood were found splattered on McCormack's motorcycle jacket. But McCormack said they must have come from an earlier meeting when he had broken up a fight between the financier and another man.

The Old Bailey jury of six men and six women deliberated all day, then were sent to a hotel for the night – with round-the-clock armed police protection. At lunchtime the following day both men were acquitted. When McCormack heard the verdict, he thanked the jury and then added: 'Come and have a drink with me over the pub.'

One elderly man in the jury winked at McCormack and raised his hand in what looked like a triumphant salute. Another observer said: 'McCormack was utterly blatant. He was grinning at the jury – and some of the jury waved and gave him the thumbs-up.'

The police were incredulous at the verdict. One detective said: 'They got to the jury. I guarantee it.' It was par for the course.

Nevertheless, an elite team from the National Crime Squad targeted the A-Team from a secret headquarters in Hertfordshire. With the help of MI5, they put Terry Adams under surveillance and bugged his house from 1997 to 1999. Alerted to this he offered to pay £95,000 in income tax. He was finally charged in 2003, but the case dragged on, partly because his wife and co-defendant Ruth suffered a perforated ulcer.

In 2007, Terry Adams pleaded guilty to one sample charge of money laundering – it was thought to keep his wife out of jail.

When he appeared at the Old Bailey, the prosecuting counsel Andrew Mitchell QC said: 'It is suggested that Terry Adams was one of the country's most feared and revered organised criminals. He comes with a pedigree, as one of a family whose name had a currency all of its own in the underworld. A hallmark of his career was his ability to keep his evidential distance from any of the violence and other crime from which he undoubtedly profited.'

Mitchell said Terry Adams had made so much money

from crime he was able to retire at the age of thirty-five. To launder his money, he had invented sham companies which he claimed to work for as a business consultant. He bought a £1 million home in North London, furnished it with antiques and paintings – some of which were stolen – and spent £78,000 on remodelling his garden.

The couple took luxury holidays, often at the Italian lakes, and bought a yacht and several cars. Their daughter, Skye, was privately educated and they also bought her a Mercedes sports car.

He was exonerated in the death of Solly Nahome.

'There is absolutely no doubt that his death came as a complete shock to Mr Adams,' said Mr Mitchell. 'But aside from the emotional impact it also had an impact on his financial affairs.'

Terry Adams was jailed for seven years. The judge made a £750,000 confiscation order and ordered him to contribute a further £50,000 towards the costs of the £1.7 million prosecution. He was joined in the dock by Mr Nahome's widow, Joanna Barnes, who admitted one charge of forgery and was fined £5,000.

Charges against Ruth Adams were allowed to 'lie on the file'. Terry gestured to her and his daughter, who were in the public gallery, as he was led away.

Alison Saunders, head of the Crown Prosecution Service's organised crime division, said: 'No-one is above the law, and where there is evidence that someone has benefited from crime in this way and has been able to establish a very comfortable lifestyle with no legitimate means of doing so, we will prosecute and will seek to confiscate those assets.'

Terry Adams was released in 2010, but the following year he was back behind bars for breaching a financial order requiring him to report all spending over £500 to police. He failed to tell them about spending sprees that included a face-lift, a Cartier watch and membership of an expensive country club for his wife.

In July 2013, Michelle Young began to stir things up again. She wrote to HMRC warning them of Young's 'criminality' and his involvement in 'tax evasion and fraud'. She was also considering a private criminal prosecution and she believed that her ex-husband was involved in money-laundering.

One of the investigators working on the case said that he felt that much of Young's money was funds held on behalf of business associates. This caused his team concern, so much so that they abandoned work on the case.

'We were concerned that all the vast wealth alleged to be Mr Young's was not, in fact, his,' he said. 'We believed he was fronting it for other people and, because it was not clear who they were, we decided not to proceed with our investigations as we were not sure who we were taking on.'

There was speculation that Young had built his fortune on devising schemes to launder money through a web of off-shore accounts. He used the money to finance huge deals, usually involving property, but sometimes buying and selling fine wines, works of art or vintage sports cars. Before the recession, the burgeoning assets market meant that the shrewdly chosen deals almost always made money for his clients, while providing ways to make the proceeds from crime or other undeclared funds legitimate.

Former business associates claimed that inventive book-keeping would even provide tax shelters for his wealthy clientele. Young would pay, say, £250,000 for a vintage Ferrari, but would record in their accounts that it cost far more. So, when the car was sold on, the profit on paper would be tiny and the large outlay could be claimed against tax. However, the sudden economic downturn caught some traders out.

Russian oligarchs who found refuge from the predations of Vladimir Putin in England were not disposed to pay what were seen internationally as Britain's punitive rates of tax on the super-rich. Alongside straightforward criminals, they would have every incentive to find ways to keep their money out of the hands of the taxman. It was said that Young and his associates would charge thirty per cent on all the money they laundered.

This would put his courtroom battle with Michelle in a different light. If the money he had salted away off-shore was money he was laundering for the Adams family, he could hardly hand half of it to his ex-wife.

Young's business was built on his reputation for trustworthiness and discretion. If he had lost money for the Adams family on Project Moscow, as well as crossing the Russian mafia, he had every reason to fear for his life. So when ex-wife Michelle started on a high-profile divorce, his business associates became understandably alarmed. Then when she hired lawyers and forensic accountants to unravel his secretive off-shore operations, he became a liability. Shortly before he died, he offered Mrs Young £30 million to bring their lengthy legal battle to an end.

Coincidentally the Adams family were back in the news about then. In February 2014, around two hundred warrants were executed in dawn raids at twenty-two addresses in London, arresting fifteen and seizing £300,000 in cash, guns, designer watches, computers and mobile phones. Among those arrested were Tommy Adams and his wife Androulla. They were released on bail.

CLOSER TO HOME

A retired Metropolitan Police detective said: 'Scotland Yard should be checking all recent contacts with Mr Young, including links to UK organised crime and Russian mafia.'

CHAPTER 21

THE LAST ROW

All theories that Young's death was connected to organised crime or the Russian mafia were put on hold when reports came out of Noelle's last row with Scot, moments before he was found dead. The story was that they had agreed to separate some time before. He had left, but then he just turned up unannounced at the flat.

'What are you doing here?' she said. 'You're not supposed to be here.'

It was said that he was manic, crazy and probably high. The situation rapidly escalated. Avoiding confrontation, she left, calling the police on the way out of the building.

'You might want to turn up,' she told them. 'There's a crazy man here. He's gone mental. He won't leave.'

Noelle then sought refuge in a girlfriend's house and when the police turned up at the apartment, they found Scot dead on the railings outside.

In the weeks before he died, Young had been drinking heavily and using cocaine. A stretch in rehab had not helped. They broke off their engagement, but they continued sharing the apartment until a few days before the fatal incident. They had even been seen out together, but he had embarrassed her socially at a number of events and often smelt of alcohol.

Their relationship had become so fraught that Noelle had insisted that he go and live elsewhere. He had left, but she had not had time to change the locks. She had been reluctant to publicise the split because of his fragile mental state. He was 'not in a good place,' she said.

A friend told *MailOnline*: 'Things were civil and they were getting along, Noelle just couldn't cope with the pressures of being with Scot – he was still very much living the millionaire's lifestyle without any of the money to back it up. Noelle couldn't continue to stand by Scot and let her own career slide. She was getting more and more offers to work in the States and was considering a move back to the US.'

Thanks to *Ladies of London* she was getting offers to do more TV in America and had been concentrating on her career plans. In the meantime, she was going back to the US for Christmas.

After having had a series of what were said to have been 'massive arguments' in recent months, the friend said the split came as a relief to both Noelle and Scot.

'It didn't sound like it was leading up to this, there was no huge drama in the past few weeks, it was more like a logical decision they both came up with,' the friend said.

The couple had split up during the week beginning 24 November, but were pictured together in public on 27 November at an opening in London to celebrate a series of photographs taken by ballet dancer Mikhail Baryshnikov.

'Although it hasn't been easy, they were still living together while Noelle worked out where she was going to move,' the same source said.

The bone of contention between Noelle and Scot was money. A friend had told her: 'It's not okay to have to pay for a fifty-two-year-old.'

Friends believed that he was being hounded for money by some rather unpleasant characters.

James Creed came to the support of the story.

'He kept phoning and phoning me on Monday,' he told the *Mail on Sunday*. 'He was in a terrible state. He told me he had booked himself into a mental institution, that he was not well but that he would be out next Thursday. He was very animated and emotional saying I was his best friend and how much he loved me. Scot was bipolar and had been in and out of clinics, he wasn't well. It was the stress of it all, he deteriorated in the past five years.'

Even so, Mr Creed did not think Young was in danger of taking his own life.

'I didn't think he was suicidal,' he said. 'He had hopes and plans for the future, he wanted to start a new life and was convinced he would make his money back.'

Plainly something had happened to precipitate the final act. David Ingram, a senior partner at accountants Grant Thornton and Young's joint trustee in bankruptcy, had spoken to him about two weeks before and recalled no hint of distress.

'He seemed fine,' Ingram said. 'He had ups and downs, but he was not particularly down when I spoke to him.'

However, Ingram knew Young had troubles.

'He had a habit, cocaine,' said the accountant. 'And there were times he came to my office smelling of alcohol. He smoked too.'

Ingram thought that might explain his death: 'For all I know he went outside for a cigarette. If he'd had a few drinks, who knows what happened?'

However, he did not appear suicidal.

'He did find Michelle's position extremely frustrating,' Ingram said. 'We know that he was living on handouts from friends. He was talking to me about getting back on his feet and we were trying to work out a plan where he would do that. He said he wanted to enter into an individual voluntary arrangement, whereby he would agree to pay back his creditors an amount he could afford. I don't think it was a secret that he had his ups and downs. He provided me with letters from doctors... that he was bipolar and he was taking medication for that. He also had a non-prescription drug habit, cocaine.'

Money laundering? 'He never particularly articulated what he was going to do... He was a deal maker, whether that was money laundering or what I don't know, but he was some-one who would set up and put deals together and then take commission,' Ingram said.

But he dismissed the 'conspiracy theories' linking Young to the Russian mafia.

'I would hope for Noelle's sake and his daughters that this was some sort of tragic accident rather than suicide,' he said. 'The danger is that they may then blame their mother; they have already lost their dad.'

Scot Young's death did not discourage Mrs Young in her relentless pursuit of her husband's lost millions. Just a week after her ex-husband had died, she was back in the High Court asking for a 'fresh pair of eyes' to run over his financial dealings. The judge ruled that she could apply for a creditors' meeting to press for the appointment of new bankruptcy trustees to carry out the search. But first she must pay outstanding costs, including those owed to the current joint trustees.

She wanted David Ingram and Richard Hicken, his partner in Grant Thornton, replaced because they had as yet uncovered none of the late Mr Young's assets. She also accused the trustees of 'lacking neutrality and being biased against her'.

Andrew Hochhauser QC, a deputy judge of the High Court's Chancery Division, confirmed Mrs Young's status as her ex-husband's largest creditor. Under the 1986 Insolvency Act, creditors have a democratic right to remove a trustee in bankruptcy at a creditors' meeting, although the courts can intervene to stop a meeting being convened.

Ingram and Hicken had applied for a direction that a meeting should not be convened, but Judge Hochhauser said: 'Mrs Young believed the bankrupt [Mr Young] to be hiding more than £400 million and certain well-known, exceptionally wealthy people were helping him to conceal his money.'

He added Family Division judge Mr Justice Moor had found the former husband had retained assets valued at £45 million, but could not say where, and the trustees had failed to find the missing money.

Judge Hochhauser concluded: 'Whilst I accept that, in all the circumstances, it is understandable that to date there has been no identification of assets belonging to the bankrupt, and I wholly reject any suggestion of reluctance or intransigence on the part of the joint trustees to identify or recover assets, Mrs Young is entitled to invite the other creditors to consider replacing the joint trustees with a "fresh pair of eyes".'

While a letter from the trustees had indicated no appetite for change, Mrs Young should have the chance to put her case, said the judge.

However, the meeting would not take place until she had

paid outstanding costs in relation to the 'unnecessary and hopeless' applications she had made to stay or annul the bankruptcy, along with the additional costs for a document production exercise carried out by the joint trustees.

While conspiracy theories over the death of Scot Young had been put on the back burner, another oligarch stepped forward to say that Young had been murdered by gangsters over a property deal. Construction magnate Valery Morozov, who fled to Britain and claimed asylum after exposing corruption in Putin's regime, told the *Sun* Young was killed by the Russian mob. He claimed Young asked mobsters to hide a rumoured £400 million fortune to keep it from his ex-wife, but they refused to return it. This explained his parlous state before he died.

A friend agreed that Young was struggling financially and had borrowed tens of thousands of pounds before he went to jail for contempt of court.

'Scot was completely broke and needed cash to tide himself over,' he said. 'There was a date set when Scot promised to pay the money back, but it came and went and then he went to prison. When Scot was released he promised he would pay him back but he repeatedly failed to do so. At one stage he offered a wristwatch as payment but the man wanted his money back.'

Morozov also alleged that the Russian secret police were interested in Young's death. Moscow gangs were, he said, 'often linked to ex-members of the Russian secret services'. They specialised in offering 'shadow business schemes' to hide owners' wealth from taxes and prying governments.

'These gangsters exploit the fact that many rich people have very limited knowledge about financial mechanisms,' he said. They grabbed hold of the companies' and the individuals' wealth. Such crimes were on the increase in Russia.

Morozov thought that Berezovsky was killed because he knew too much about these schemes used by the super-rich; and Young was murdered for similar reasons.

'I know that Young was also linked to Berezovsky,' said Morozov who made his allegations from hiding. 'I have information that Russian law enforcement agencies have paid close attention to Young's murder. He had similar problems – he declared he had no money but in reality it was hidden and our gangs have a lot to do with it. In my opinion, Young may have become a victim of such a gang, and probably this is why Moscow police are interested in his death.'

In a long interview with *MailOnline*, Morozov said: 'Many people in Russia are convinced that Boris Berezovsky was murdered. And one version is that he was murdered exactly because he knew all about these off-shores and trusts abroad which are controlled by Russian gangs and earn millions of dollars to all those involved in these schemes. It is a huge industry and Berezovsky knew it well.'

Morozov explained that such corruption was not a recent phenomenon in Russia.

'The reason why Berezovsky and his associates climbed up so quickly in the 1990s lies in the same area – they were dealing with the money transfers for Boris Yeltsin. Later, many gangs were shaped around this core. They call themselves legal companies which offer their services in running off-shores. Imagine a Russian official who stole the money and did not pay taxes, and he seeks help in running an off-shore company to take care of his wealth.'

Corrupt officials were in league with gangsters and specialists in hiding money off-shore such as Scot Young.

'These off-shore management companies can build it up in a way that the official will be convinced he is still in charge of the money,' Morozov said. 'But one day the money is gone and he can't prove anything. He can't go to court because it will ask about the origin of his money. He has no choice, but if he still does not want to keep a low profile, he is killed.'

Murder was the stock-in-trade of Russians who hide their ill-gotten gains off-shore.

'These crimes are to do with the companies and their money kept off-shore,' said Morozov. 'The most frequent crime is the quiet replacement of the owner in an off-shore company. A gang makes friends with the owner of an off-shore, gains his trust, volunteers to run his off-shore for him in a way that the owner poorly controls it. Then the owner suddenly finds that – through the murky trails needed to keep identities secret – he no longer has control of his own company.'

That could have been the fate of Scot Young.

Another Russian divorcee who had been dragged through the Royal Courts of Justice suffered a similar fate, according to Morozov. The Russian millionaire, described only as 'shady puppet master', had met his wife in 1987 in a Russian factory where they both worked. They married in 1991 and had two children together. In 2005 they moved to Britain, where they lived in a £3.8 million home in central London and enjoyed a 'lavish lifestyle'.

The wife, who was not named due to reporting restrictions, divorced her husband in Russia in 2009 and went on to apply for a financial settlement at the High Court in London, where Mrs Justice Eleanor King strongly criticised the wealthy businessman for refusing to co-operate with the legal proceedings and being in contempt of court 'many times over'. She called the case 'a fantastic charade'.

'At fabulous cost – £1.4 million and counting – those represent-ing the wife have crossed and re-crossed the globe in an attempt to trace the husband's assets, every penny of which has been acquired during the course of the marriage,' the judge said.

The wife's QC put the husband's known assets at about £107 million, made up of eleven commercial properties in Russia and eight properties in England.

The judge ruled that this should be split fifty-fifty with the wife and awarded her £53,531,168, including a lump sum of £38 million.

'The husband was the wealth creator, the wife the home-maker,' said the judge. 'Each contributed fully to the marriage. I am satisfied that all the family's wealth was created during the course of the marriage.'

However, Mrs Justice Eleanor King admitted that the wife would face 'very substantial costs' in enforcing the settlement against her husband. Indeed, she was left in a situation not dissimilar to that of Mrs Young.

Morozov then explained the fate of the Russian divorcé.

'He lived in London for a long time,' he said, 'then went back to Russia and was surprised to discover that his off-shore companies do not belong to him any more but to somebody else.'

He died when twenty-seven bullets hit his car.

'He was murdered because he got to know about it too early and too suddenly,' said Morozov. 'But he was likely to be murdered anyway, sooner or later.'

Was he another in the Ring of Death? Morozov also claimed to have information that Russian law enforcement agencies were linking his murder to Berezovsky's death.

But it was not just corruption in Russia that was to blame. Morozov said that the authorities in the West were turning a blind eye to this wrong-doing as it helped to destabilise the increasingly belligerent Russian state.

'The West likes to talk about corruption in Russia,' he said. 'But the financial centre of this corruption is located exactly in the West. Recently it started drifting to the East because of sanctions. The money is taken away from Russia and moves from one company to another.'

With the collapse of the rouble, more Russian oligarchs were pouring into the UK as they had more than enough cash to buy visas.

'British people are making a serious mistake when they do not consider that many Russian newcomers have a criminal background,' warned Morozov. 'For many it became enough to say that they are against Putin, and they automatically became friends of the West. This way of thinking comes from Soviet times and Russian criminals use it. Having settled in the West, such gangsters continue running their shadow criminal business via off-shores.'

Morozov's own life was once thought to have been in danger after the body of forty-four-year-old Alexander Perepilichny was found outside his home in Weybridge, Surrey, in November 2012. He had been helping Swiss prosecutors in a money-laundering case involving Russian officials, provoking suspicion an 'invisible' poison may have been used to kill him. The detectives investigating Perepilichny's death asked Morozov whether he believed his own life was in danger.

Perepilichny had fled to Britain in 2009 after falling out with his business partners and being told by the police that his name had appeared on a mob hit-list. The following year, he handed the Swiss authorities documents concerning a money-laundering scheme defrauding the Russian treasury of $220 million. This had initially been exposed by lawyer Sergei Magnitsky, who subsequently died in police custody in Moscow in 2009 after being beaten and apparently refusing medical treatment. The roll call of Russian officials who were denied US visas and had their assets frozen because they were thought to be involved in Magnitsky's death was known as the 'Magnitsky List'.

To start with, Surrey Police thought that Mr Perepilichny's death was not suspicious, but concerns grew later. However, two autopsies were inconclusive and advanced toxicology tests proved negative.

'It was the same policemen who arrested and jailed Magnitsky that now cover the bureaucrats and get bribes from them, as well as act as cover for various tax affairs,' said Magnitsky. 'This is why I have to be answering various police questions: "What do you know about Perepilichny's death? Why are Magnitsky and Perepilichny dead – and you are alive? Do you consider your life to be in danger?" I answer them. But they ask again – "What about on a ten-point scale, where is the risk?" I say, five.'

Morozov himself had blown the whistle on corruption at the Winter Olympics at Sochi and fled for his life, claiming he had become a 'marked man'. He had claimed that Vladimir Putin's office in Moscow had demanded huge pay-offs from people who wanted construction contracts for the stadiums and other facilities at the 2014 winter games. These were paid direct to a Kremlin official. Morozov knew this because, as a building contractor, pay-offs had been demanded from him. He said that he had personally delivered 'tens of millions of roubles' in cash bribes. He left for the UK with a price on his head after being told by gangsters: 'You will be drowned in blood.'

CHAPTER 22

THE SUICIDE CLUB

Exiled construction magnate Valery Morozov knew a lot more than what was going on in the underworld of construction in Russia. He had also been privy to the goings-on in London where, he said, Scot Young was a member of a secretive society called the 'Suicide Club'. Its motto was: 'It's easy to make money, but hard to spend it with maximum pleasure.'

The other members of this exclusive dining club were Boris Berezovsky, Johnny Elichaoff, Paul Castle and Robert Curtis.

'They were united by a love of money, delicious food and expensive wines, cognac and whiskies,' Morozov said. 'They were also united by the fact that all of them were very rich. All of them followed Berezovsky's advice and invested in property in Russia. And one more thing unites all of them. All turned out to be suicides, according to London police.'

Despite dubbing their fraternity the Suicide Club, Morozov

did not believe that they had killed themselves. There was a more sinister explanation.

'Within the last four years all of them stopped eating, drinking and meeting,' he said. 'All the deaths were called non-suspicious, excluding Berezovsky. The other deaths look innocent. Only with Young, it is not that simple. Before his death he complained of threats. But if we look at what they invested in Russia, the picture turns out to be very strange.'

All of them were experienced businessmen, but in Russia they found themselves out of their depth and they had made a huge mistake.

'They were not stupid fools, but each of them transferred dozens of millions of dollars into a project we can hardly find any trace of,' said Morozov.

He said the original purpose of the Project Moscow deal was to launder money for the mafia and their associates in Britain. Ostensibly the scheme involved 'some kind of office building on the land of a paint factory,' said Mr Morozov. 'But there is no way to find any trace of it. And in order to make a sensible investor pay upfront for a property which does not exist, avoiding help from his lawyers and financial advisers, you need very strange circumstances and extremely good reasons for the investor himself. There were no documents, no project, no business plan. Why did they pay?'

Morozov said that there was only one explanation.

'You pay according to such a scheme only in one case – the money must disappear and the project must collapse. In other words, the money must turn up somewhere where nobody would find it, and this money must be in a place nobody would know about. Sometimes, even those who pay, know nothing.'

Such a scheme involves a certain amount of trust, but Young and his circle trusted the wrong people.

THE SUICIDE CLUB

'The members of this Suicide Club had been hiding their money in off-shore structures via Russia and Russian business projects,' Morozov said. 'This is the only sensible explanation. Every member of this club stopped living when they officially had no money.'

Not only were they in bed with the Russian mafia, they were also dealing with corrupt officials who could paper over the cracks.

'All the members of Suicide Club were sort of "sluice covers", used to hide money from corrupt officials in Russia who topped up their own investments,' he said. 'Via this sluice the money was going from Russia to off-shores. This is why there is a difference between the personal wealth of each club member and the amount of money which was transferred via the sluice.'

For example, Young's estimated wealth was a maximum of £400–500 million. However, it was reported that he transferred £2 billion into one of these so-called projects in Russia. Once the money had been 'invested', Young no longer had control of it. He had been out-manoeuvred by Russian gangs who were linked to the country's secret services.

Morozov said all five of the 'Suicide Club' members lost money on Russian investments hidden in off-shore companies in the same way.

'Since the beginning of the 1990s, the Western criminal world started using ex-KGB employees and Russian criminal structures, controlled by secret services, in order to build up and improve the world system of money laundering for criminal money,' Morozov said. 'In the world there is a strong and secret system of transferring, hiding and legalising criminal money from the ex-USSR and other former socialist countries.'

Other Russian sources suggest that the shock of finding his

money had vanished drove Young to despair, depression and suicide. That might also have been the fate of other members of the Suicide Club. They simply did not know who they were getting involved with.

According to diplomatic cables released by Wikileaks in December 2010, Russia is a 'virtual mafia state'. The political establishment, including prime minister Vladimir Putin, was in cahoots with the oligarchs and organised crime to profit from arms trafficking, money laundering, protection rackets, extortion and other kickbacks. According to the leaked US cables, bribery alone was running at an estimated $300 billion a year. Suitcases full of money find their way to secret off-shore bank accounts in Cyprus and it was often hard to distinguish between the activities of the government and the Russian mafia.

Law enforcement agencies including the police, state security and the prosecutor's office actively protect the criminal networks within the country. Russian spy agencies use mafia bosses to carry out criminal operations such as arms trafficking. Unbridled bribery acted like a parallel tax system for the enrichment of policemen, officials and officers of the KGB's successor, the federal security service (FSB). The cables accused Putin himself of amassing money from his time in office, which is hidden overseas.

Organised crime sprang up in Russia before the collapse of Communism. It began in 1988 when the Soviet Union began to allow private enterprise, without putting in place the laws to control a market economy that exist in the West. A market opened next to Rizhsky Railway Station in Moscow was taken over by street hooligans. As central control collapsed, corrupt officials hived off state enterprises for their personal gain. Veterans of the KGB and the Afghan and Chechen wars found themselves out of work and turned to crime.

THE SUICIDE CLUB

By 1993, most of the banks were owned by the Russian mafia and over three-quarters of businesses were paying protection money. Kidnapping, bombing and gangland slayings soared. That year, 1,400 people were murdered in Moscow. Criminals had no compunction in killing businessmen who would not pay protection, or bank owners, politicians or journalists who opposed them. According to the whistleblower Alexander Litvinenko, the biggest criminal cartel was formed by former KGB men. He called it the Lubyanka Gang, after the KGB's headquarters in Lubyanka Square. Members included former KGB officer Vladimir Putin. He was associated with the property company SPAG, thought to have been used by St Petersburg mobsters to launder money.

Through the KGB's overseas contacts, the Russian mafia went international, controlling the drug traffic out of Afghanistan and making connections with the Sicilian Cosa Nostra, the Chinese Triads and the Latin American drug cartels. They also set up an operation in the Brighton Beach area of Brooklyn in the US. However, in 1997, the head of the New York operation, Vyacheslav Ivankov, also known as Yaponchik or 'Little Japanese', was convicted in a $5.6-million extortion case. Thanks to mass emigration, the Russian mafia has also taken over the underworld in Israel with Russian gangsters producing bogus proof of Jewish ancestry to settle there.

Like organised crime in America, the Russian mafia was not a single entity. It was split into a number of individual gangs. The Izmaylovskaya gang from the Izmaylovo District it thought to be the oldest and most important mafia group in Moscow. It also had tentacles in Tel Aviv, Berlin, Paris, Toronto, Miami and New York City. With quasi-military ranks and strict internal discipline, it was involved in extortion and murder-for-hire, and had infiltrated legitimate businesses. There were accusations that it made $250 million out of one protection racket alone.

The Solnsevskaya Brotherhood operated out of the Solntsevo district of Moscow. It was involved in money laundering, prostitution, credit card fraud, human trafficking, arms dealing and other illegal activities. It also had a presence in Toronto and San Francisco, and was thought to have over five thousand members. In the 1990s, it merged with the Orekhovskaya gang to counter the encroachment of the Chechen mafia. In 2005, eleven of its members were sentenced to up to twenty-four years for eighteen brutal murders.

The Tambov gang had taken over businesses in St Petersburg. In 2008, members were arrested in Spain, Bulgaria and Berlin. The police operations in Spain also bagged $307,000 in cash and twenty-three luxury cars, and froze twelve million euros in bank accounts there. The Bulgarian prosecutor said that more than one billion euros from drug trafficking, prostitution and protect rackets had been laundered through Estonia and Bulgaria. More dirty money was laundered in Berlin.

Crime gangs had also sprung up in other parts of the former Soviet Union. The Potato Bag gang were a bunch of con-men from Odessa who operated among the émigré community in Brighton Beach. The largest of the non-Russian gangs is the Chechen mafia who, as well as drug trafficking, have links to Islamic fundamentalists.

In the 1990s, the Russian mafia also infiltrated the Afghan veterans' association – the Russian equivalent of the British Legion or America's Vietnam Veterans Association. Its head was murdered and the association split into two factions. The head of one branch, Valery Radchikov, survived an assassination attempt in 1995. The following year, the leader of the other faction, Sergei Trakhirov, his wife and eleven others were killed when a bomb exploded in a cemetery during a funeral. There were of course funds intended for veterans, ready and waiting to be embezzled, held by both factions.

While police forces in other countries tried their best to keep the Russian mafia in check, the authorities back home in Russia make no attempt to stem the growth of organised crime. With the Cosa Nostra having it wings clipped both in Sicily and the US, the Russian mafia had ambitions to take over. And what better place to start than London, the centre of world banking where numerous corrupt oligarchs already lived?

CHAPTER 23

THE DUNDEE CONNECTION

Just two weeks after his demise, another mysterious death came to light that had connections to Scot Young. And it stretched all the way back to his early career in Dundee.

On 21 December 2014, the Glasgow *Sunday Mail* made the connection between Scot Young and his old boss, Dundee pub and casino boss Alex Brown – the sixty-year-old's body had been found floating near his luxury yacht in the harbour at Port de Sóller, Majorca, in 2006 – coincidentally around the time Young was going bust. Although the cause of death was given as drowning, police also looked into claims from Brown's family that he may have been murdered after he was seen arguing with a man on the harbour's edge.

Former casino manager for the Scottish–Greek Cypriot hotel magnate and casino owner Reo Stakis, Brown ran some of Dundee's most successful pubs and clubs in the 1980s and 1990s, including McGonagall's, Café American and Jacques nightclub in Broughty Ferry. Young worked for Brown in his pub business in the early to mid 1980s and lived in a flat owned by Brown above McGonagall's in the city. Apparently, this was where Young learnt his trade.

'He enjoyed hanging about with older businessmen like Brown in the city and picking their brains,' a prominent Dundee businessman told the *Mail*. 'As far as I know he never had a job but he was never short of money. I think he was the gofer type who would be used by Brown for various tasks.'

Like Young, Brown had a darker side. He escaped charges of attempted murder after he had pulled a shotgun on a stranger in Dundee after a drunken argument. Several of his pubs mysteriously caught fire and he was made bankrupt in 1994 over the debts of a shop-fitting firm. Released from bankruptcy in 2000, with most of his assets in the names of his wife Margot and sons, he moved to Spain where he ran the Café Pacific on Majorca.

Café Pacific was a popular bar with both British expats and tourists. It showed live football and rugby on a wide-screen TV and Port de Sóller was a friendly, family-orientated resort. The Browns lived in a £120,000 first-floor flat in a private block, with an outdoor swimming pool, five minutes' drive from the bar. He drove a green Jeep Cherokee.

At the time of his death, the island's police insisted there were no suspicious circumstances. However, his family persuaded authorities to allow a second post-mortem after reports of the heated row on the quayside with a mystery man. This led to the case being reopened.

Jim Ross, who used to run McGonagall's with Brown, told the *Sunday Mail*: 'Alex was too lucky for anything like an accident ever to happen to him. My money would be on something else having happened.'

Like Young, Brown had a glittering business career behind him.

'During the 1980s, he was right at the top of his game,' said Ross. 'He seemed to have the Midas touch – but he had a low boredom threshold and lost interest in things quickly. I don't know much about his business dealings because I didn't want to get involved. I did know that the people around him always got into trouble whereas he seemed to end up OK.'

On the night he died, he shut Café Pacific at 1.30 am as he was planning to leave the next morning for a long sailing holiday with his wife. They were going to sail off nearby Ibiza on their 32-foot yacht *Soutar*. As he left the bar, he had handed the keys to his Swedish business partner who was going to run the place while he was away. Then he headed out for a late-night drink to celebrate.

Brown was pleased to be leaving as there had been trouble at Café Pacific that afternoon. He had been involved in a row with a group of Englishmen.

Ramon Lopez, the owner of a neighbouring bar, said: 'I heard there was an argument or a fight with some British men in Café Pacific on the Saturday afternoon. That's unusual as Port de Sóller is pretty quiet. We don't attract the yob element other resorts get. Alex was well known and popular in Sóller. I count him as a friend and we had many drinks together.'

However, there was a second row after Brown had locked up and moved on to the nearby St Tropez bar. He was playing pool and drinking vodka in the basement when a row broke out around 4.30 am.

'Alex was pretty drunk,' said a fellow drinker. 'He was playing pool and got into a shouting match with a local Spanish guy, a chef at a nearby hotel. They were squaring up and the barman

Tony had to step in to stop it kicking off. In the end, the local guy left the bar and Alex calmed down.'

Brown left Saint Tropez with a British friend around 5 am and walked down towards the harbour. His friend went off home while Brown said he was heading for another late-night disco bar called Altamar. There he seems to have run into more trouble. A police source said: 'We have been told of a third fight with someone he had been enemies with for some time.'

At 7.30 am, he was found floating face down in the harbour by fifteen-year-old Xisco Blau, a fisherman's son.

However, there was more to this than a local tiff. Brown was a man of action and was not entirely happy with his life in the sun.

A friend told the *Mail*: 'Alex was a bit fed up running the Pacific. It wasn't as busy as he would have hoped and they thought by changing the management they could up the takings. He was talking about it in the bar the night before he died, saying he was going to take [his wife] Margote to Ibiza on the boat for a long holiday.'

Plainly he was considering his future.

'He loved sailing his boat and fishing and was really looking forward to a retirement without having to work every day,' his friend said.

Local police first thought the bar owner had wandered off to his boat and drowned in the harbour after suffering a heart attack. But Margote and sons Christopher and Nicholas told the police that they thought the circumstance of his death were suspicious. The family accused the police of jumping to conclusions, even though an autopsy showed no signs of a violent death. The cremation that was due to take place just four days after his death was stopped by a judge who ordered a second autopsy. He also ordered the Civil Guard, the national police force, to take over the investigation.

THE DUNDEE CONNECTION

They issued a statement, saying: 'We are investigating thoroughly the claims by Mr Brown's family that foul play may have played a part in his death. We take these claims very seriously. We are aware of the various reports of arguments and are interviewing anybody who saw or spoke to Mr Brown on the night of his death.'

Even so, six months later it was ruled that he had died from accidental drowning. Brown was known to be a heavy drinker. The mysterious man he was seen arguing with on the harbour's edge has never been identified.

CHAPTER 24

THE INQUEST ADJOURNED

When the inquest into Scot Young's death opened on 23 December 2014, the authorities were still saying that it was 'not foul play'. Detectives dismissed claims that the bankrupt entrepreneur died as part of a plot involving his connections to Russian oligarchs, the court heard.

Coroner's officer Rosalind Tolson confirmed Scot's body was found 'impaled on railings' and there were no suspicious circumstances.

The public gallery was packed when Angela Hodes, Westminster assistant coroner, said: 'Mr Young was found impaled on railings outside 33 Montagu Square, Marylebone, with multiple injuries and was confirmed dead at the scene. Police are not treating his death as suspicious.'

The body was identified by his brother-in-law Guy van Ristell, while his daughter Sasha gave details to police. None of Scot's family or friends was at the hearing, which lasted barely two minutes. Adjourning the inquest, the assistant coroner said: 'I will open the inquest touching the death of Scot Guy Young who died on 8 December and I will adjourn that for a coroner's review on 12 January 2015.'

The family had already been told that the body would not be released until the New Year. Usually when a body is not released, it means that a post-mortem examination is being carried out in case there is to be a criminal investigation into a death.

It was also reported that Noelle visited Scot's two daughters to offer her condolences, before returning to the US for Christmas and to await further news. In an interview, Noelle said that Scot had a good relationship with his daughters after the split. They refused to go public about the matter, but those who spoke to them got the impression that 'Ms Reno had misinterpreted the relationship.'

It then emerged that Young had discharged himself from a NHS mental health unit just hours before his fall. He had twice been sectioned under the Mental Health Act and was taking prescription medication for bipolar disorder. Being followed by the private investigators his ex-wife had put on the case – and, perhaps, others – had left him paranoid.

'In the condition I am in, paranoia can manifest in many ways, especially when you have eight people following you,' he said. 'I spent fourteen days in hospital under the Mental Health Act... It was not a nice experience.'

On 5 December, he had admitted himself to the Gordon Hospital in central London. The unit specialises in treating severe mental health problems. Its website says it only admits patients who are 'in an acute phase of a serious mental illness'. But Mr Young walked out on 8 December. This time he had not been sectioned so hospital staff could not force him to stay.

Hours later, he showed up at his ex-girlfriend's apartment. When she walked out, he phoned, warning he was going to jump. Health workers were obliged to check on him within twenty-four hours but he was dead by the time they called.

James Creed told the *Daily Mail*: 'He was in a mental home. He was in the same place two years ago, it's a horrible place. He called me when he was there every day. Then he called me on the Monday and said he was coming out. I don't know why.'

A spokesman for Central and North West London NHS Foundation Trust said: 'We are also investigating his care and his mutually agreed discharge from the ward to home.'

Nobody was around when Scot Young died – or, at least, no one who has come forward. So it looks as if the mystery will endure. It is true that he was mentally disturbed at the time. But the origin of that disturbance is not known.

He complained of being paranoid. But then Mrs Young had private detectives and other investigators following him and prying into every aspect of his life; and there are indications that he may have made enemies among gangsters – British, or Russian, or both. The Kremlin also exhibited an extraordinary interest in his death, so maybe the Russian secret police were on his tail.

One would have reason enough to be a little paranoid if four close friends in the same line of business had died in mysterious ways. Friends also expressed the opinion that Scot had been hounded to death. But had he been hounded by criminal associates or legitimate creditors – or was it Mrs Young they were referring to?

She had every reason to pursue him for a fair share of the money that had been built up in their life together. And it is a legitimate question to ask why he would rather go to jail than reveal anything about where it had gone – and why he felt safer in jail than out. Surely, out on the streets, he was not fearful of her. So whom was he scared of?

When it comes to his death, the question is first left with the coroner. But coroner's inquests get adjourned and delayed. The process can take years. Maybe not as many years as the divorce case took. Nobody could afford that. Justice delayed is justice denied. But it can drag on. Most inquests do. And then they can come to an 'open verdict'. No one is to blame, it might have been an accident, no one is sure. Of course, it is not the job of a coroner's court to investigate, only to listen to the evidence presented. Just as you, the reader, have sifted through what I have unearthed.

As taxpayers, we pay the authorities to do that. Maybe those who have spent their lives avoiding tax don't deserve such treatment. But that can't be true. No matter how high the elevated lives the super-rich live are above us, they affect our lives too. If they pay less tax, I pay more. If their money finances political parties, the less the parties care about my paltry vote. I can't afford a billboard, or a party political broadcast, or the money to back the campaign to elect the leader of a political party. Some people can.

Not that I resent the influence these entrepreneurs have. Plainly, they are cleverer than me, or the rest of us, to have made all that money. And money is the water all us little fishes swim through. But it is a dilemma for all of us. What would you do if you won the lottery – which in many ways is what Scot Young had done?

Sure, it would be wonderful to live in a massive mansion, waited on by servants and have the full Downton-Abbey lifestyle. But I don't play the lottery because, if I won, perhaps I would be dead within a month – with all those drugs and prostitutes. And gratefully so. I have always made my living, from day to day, week to week, month to month, by hustling for book commissions, then fulfilling them – satisfactorily, I hope. That is not what I do, it is who I am. Without having to do that, I am not sure I have any identity.

That is the key here. What was Scot Young? Who was he? What were his goals? How did he define himself? Without money, he became a shadow of his former self. He was a ghost.

The truth is, Scot Young died as he lived – a mystery. He hid his wealth – and, perhaps, the wealth of others – behind a thick forest of bogus companies and sham accounts in off-shore havens. He did not commit records to paper or even, much, to computer disk. The details of his dealings were in his head. They have died with him. Those who helped salt his money away are hardly likely to come forward with it now. One can only hope that enough can be unearthed to save his ex-wife and daughters from any further hardship. As for Scot, he had his day in the sun.

And Noelle Reno? Surely she is destined for stardom.